God Magnified, Part 7

Surveying the Economy
of the Kingdom

By Eric Mumford

LIFECHANGERS®

P.O. Box 3709 ❖ Cookeville, TN 38502
931.520.3730 ❖ lc@lifechangers.org

The Scripture quotations contained in this book are from:
    The New American Standard Bible®, Copyright © 1960, 1962, 1963, 1971, 1972, 1973, 1975, 1977, 1995 by The Lockman Foundation. *The Amplified Bible.* 1987. La Habra, CA: The Lockman Foundation.

PLUMBLINE

Published by:

LIFECHANGERS ®
LIBRARY SERIES

P.O. Box 3709 | Cookeville, TN 38502
(800) 521-5676 | www.lifechangers.org

Contents

God Magnified Statements
14 Pillars of the Trinity's Dwelling Place

Pillar 1 | God is an "**Us**"– three Individuals (Gen. 1:26, 3:22, 11:7; Isa. 6:8).

Pillar 2 | "God is **One**" (Deut. 6:4; Mark 12:29).

Pillar 3 | "God is **Love (*Agape*)**" (1 John 4:8, 16).

Pillar 4 | "God is a **sun**" (Psa. 84:11).

Pillar 5 | "**Holy, Holy, Holy** is the Lord God, the Almighty" (Rev. 4:8; Isa. 6:3).

Pillar 6 | "God is **Light**" (1 John 1:5).

Pillar 7 | "The eternal God is a **dwelling place**" (Deut. 33:27).

Pillar 8 | "God **in Christ**" (Col. 2:9; 2 Cor. 5:19; Eph. 4:32).

Pillar 9 | "God is **spirit**" (John 4:24).

Pillar 10 | "God is **true**" (John 3:33).

Pillar 11 | "God Most High" (Ps. 78:35; Heb. 7:1).

Pillar 12 | "The Lord is a God of **justice**" (Isa. 30:18).

Pillar 13 | "The Lord, whose name is *Jealous*, is a **jealous** God" (Ex. 34:14).

Pillar 14 | "God is a **consuming fire**" (Deut. 4:24; Heb. 12:29).

Pillar 15 | God is three sacrificial **Self-sharers** (Eph. 4:7-10).

God Magnified, Part 6
Surveying the Economy
of the Kingdom

By Eric Mumford

Introduction

In this *Plumbline* series, we are discovering the "**dwelling place**," which the Persons of the Trinity not only *share* but which the three Eternals *are*. Before the heavens and the earth or any created being existed, the "eternal **Father**" (Isa. 9:6), the "eternal **Son**" (1 Tim. 1:16-17; John 1:1), and the "eternal **Spirit**" (Heb. 9:14), *Themselves* constituted "the **eternal kingdom**" (2 Pet. 1:11). God is three relational, Self-giving Persons who *mutually indwell* One Another. The Triune-God is profoundly inclusive and hospitable; into this relational, inter-Personal infrastructure, known as the kingdom of God, we have been invited. The Triune-God is calling us Home into Themselves: *re-gene-rating*, fusing, and acculturating us as adopted children into **God in Christ**.

The *God is* or God magnified statements of the Scriptures are like pillars of a covered porch built around the entire circumference of **God is a dwelling place**; each pillar serves as a lens to see and understand the next truth about God. Progressive magnification of these *God is* declarations leads to a three-dimensional understanding of the eternal kingdom and draws us to enter and participate through the God-Man Jesus in the *eternal life* of the Triune-God. As kingdom emigrants, we are pioneering forward together into this unfolding revelation of **the fusion of the Trinity**.

In the previous volume, *God Magnified Part 6: Appraising the Most High*, we discovered that Father, Son, and Spirit are, together, "the Most High God" (Ps. 78:35; Heb. 7:1). These three humble Eternals perpetually exalt One Another. We examined the universal law that issues forth from the nature of the Triune-God Themselves: "Whoever **exalts himself** [*eros: self-worth-ship*] shall be humbled; and whoever humbles himself [*Agape: self-emptying*] shall be exalted" (Matt. 23:12). The dynamic movement of the kingdom of God can be described as a *downward ascent* because all the individuals participating in it humble themselves as burden-bearers to sacrificially lift one another—"the building up of one another" (Rom. 14:19). The fall of man into self-worth-ship and self-exaltation is a contrary movement—an *upward descent*. The first shall be last is an upward descent.

We also discovered that the Scriptures use **economic terms** to describe how these three Eternals *add to* and *exalt* One Another by sacrificial Self-giving in reciprocal *gene-rosity*. The economy of the kingdom functions by **giving and receiving** in order to give again, which yields superabundant bounty (Phil.

4:15). The archangel Lucifer was the first to fall into self-worth-ship and *sell* his inheritance in God Most High: "By the **abundance of your trade** [*exchanging economies*] you were internally filled with violence" (Ezek. 28:16). In *upward descent*, Lucifer became "Belial" [*lit.* ***Worthless***] (2 Cor. 6:15) and "the father of lies" (John 8:44)—a dirt-dweller and a predatory opportunist.

Human beings **fell** out of the *abundant life* of the Most High because we "**exchanged** the truth of God [*relational altruism*] for a lie [*eros individualism*], and worshipped and served the creature [*self-worth-ship*] rather than the Creator [*the "Us" of our genesis*]" (Rom. 1:25). We bought into Worthless' world economy that operates by **buying and selling** one another for self-indulgence, which precipitates famine. As **dispirited dirt-bags,**[1] we were filled with the *de-gene-rate* nature, insatiable desire, and corrupt rationale of the false-father. We have become *acculturated* into Worthless' marketplace; he has *mentored* us as predatory opportunists who restlessly "pant after the very dust of the earth" (Amos 2:7) seeking to build an empire of dirt. The "things above" (Col. 3:1-2) or relational, inter-personal life and economy of the Triune-Most High remain **eclipsed** to us.

---

[1] "We have this treasure in earthen vessels" (2 Cor. 4:7). We were born dirt bags, created from dust and ash. Dispirited dirt bags lack even someone to guide or lead them. A redeemed dirt bag contains and grows the Eternal Seed producing bounty. See Matt. 9:36; Gen. 3:19, 18:27.

In this volume, *Surveying the Economy of the Kingdom*, we will see how "**Jesus, Son of the Most High God**" (Luke 8:28) came down to us as captives in our *fallen* state of individualism to pierce through our **eclipse** and embody and reveal in Himself "the mysteries of the kingdom of heaven" (Matt. 13:11). In the God-Man Jesus Christ, the Triune-God seeks to *lift* us into Themselves by mentoring us in **kingdom economics** that we might become "**sons** [*and daughters*] **of the Most High**" (Luke 6:35).

The Kingdom Eclipsed, Lost and Forgotten

The transcendent reality of God Most High is **obscured** by individualism and self-exaltation. Self-love **eclipses** true Love because "the arrogance of your heart has deceived you" (Obad. 1:3). Paul said it this way, "If anyone thinks he is **something** [*inherently special, a self-center worthy to be added to and served*] when he is **nothing** [*an inebriated, dispirited dirt-bag filled with Worthless' ashes*], he **deceives himself** [*he has bought into the lie of self-worth-ship*]" (Gal. 6:3). The more we become *acculturated* into Worthless' world—*mature* in his rationale *investing* in his corrupt marketplace, actively *mentored* by the false-father as hypocrites, counterfeiters, and opportunists, especially as religious people—the more complete our **eclipse** becomes from the fusion glory of God Most High. Jesus said, "Blessed are the **pure** in heart [*lit. Greek:*

katharos—purified by fire; e.g. eros-free, purged from desiring desire], for they shall **see** God" (Matt. 5:8).

> [11]Jesus answered them, "To you [*who recognize and follow Me: God in Christ*] it has been granted to know the **mysteries of the kingdom of heaven** [*relational dynamic of God Most High: Father, Son, and Spirit in fusion Oneness by reciprocal gene-rosity and mutual exaltation*], but to them [*who seek to save their autonomous life*] it has not been granted. [12]For **whoever has** [*e.g. bought into the God-Man Nucleus by losing his life*], **to him shall more be given**, and he will have an **abundance** [*gene-rative bounty*]; but **whoever does not have** [*exchanges the truth for the lie*], even what he has shall be **taken away** from him [*famine*]. [13]Therefore I speak to them [*individualists*] in parables [*veiled teachings*]; because while seeing they **do not see** [*"suppress the truth in unrighteousness" Rom. 1:18*], and while hearing they **do not hear**, **nor do they understand** [*eclipsed by desiring desire, mammon, self-worth-ship*]" (Matt. 13:11-13).

The economy of the kingdom is "whoever has, to him shall more be given" and the economy of the world is "whoever does not have, even what he has shall be taken away from him" (vs. 12). Due to our preoccupation with building an empire of dirt, the *spiritual* quality of life, which Father, Son, and Spirit *share* and eagerly desire to *share* with us, has been lost or hidden in the realm of secret mystery. "**The things above**" (Col. 3:1) that ought to be so *familiar* are now altogether *foreign*. Like Tarzan, raised and mentored by animals, we have become so *accustomed* to our life in **exile** that we have **forgotten our true origin**—our *true* father is *the Earl of Greystoke* and we are the heir of his vast estate.

From time to time, we may feel the heat and power of the Light of the glory of God in Christ on our faces, yet blinded by self-focus, we individualists cannot see it. We are all born with a corrupt, fallen nature, but participating in Worthless' economy causes us to sink deeper in the mud: "For everyone who **exalts** himself [*self-worth-ship*] will be humbled [*upward descent*], and he who humbles himself [*acknowledges "I am but dust and ashes" Gen. 18:27*] will be **exalted** [*lifted from the ash heap, re-gene-rated, and received into God Most High*]" (Luke 14:11). David wrote: "They [*who awaken to God Most High*] will sing of the ways of the Lord [*altruism: reciprocal Agape, mutual exaltation, downward ascent*], for great is the glory of the Lord [*fusion of the Trinity in the Nucleus of Christ*]. For though the Lord is **exalted** [***Triune-Most High***], yet He regards the lowly [*self-emptied*], but the haughty [*self-worth-shippers, individualists*] He knows from afar (Ps. 138:5-6).

This relational estrangement between God and human beings has two sides: *our* **willful fission** from God in autonomy, suspicion, and seeking our own desire and the distance *God* experiences in **repulsion** to our arrogant self-exaltation. God certainly knows and loves individualists, but He knows us "from afar." Through Isaiah, God explained this *repulsion*:

> [12]When you come to appear before Me [*as takers, opportunists*], who requires of you this **trampling** of My courts [*violating the sacred nest of vulnerable rest as pretenders*]? [13]Bring your **worthless offerings** no longer [*Agape with hypocrisy*]...I cannot endure iniquity and the solemn assembly [*profaning precious relationships with worthless intentions*].... [15]So when you spread out your hands in prayer, **I will hide My eyes from you**... (Isa. 1:12-15).

God called Jeremiah to fellowship in His sufferings by remaining *faithful* to his *faithless* people. Known as "the weeping prophet," Jeremiah despaired of life *cohabiting* with those who had invested themselves into Worthless' marketplace: "Oh that I had in the desert a wayfarers' lodging place; that I may leave my people and go from them! For all of them are adulterers, **an assembly of treacherous men** [*opportunists in confusion*]" (Jer. 9:2). God added:

.

³"They bend their tongue like their bow; **lies and not truth prevail** in the land [*a crab bucket ²*]; for they proceed **from evil to evil** [*rather than "from glory to glory"; maturing in corruption*], and **they do not know Me** [*eclipsed from God Most High*]," declares the Lord. ⁴"Let everyone be on his guard against his neighbor, and do not trust [*invest in*] any brother; because every brother deals **craftily** [*Agape with hypocrisy*], and every neighbor goes about as a **slanderer** [*devouring with words*]. ⁵Everyone **deceives** his neighbor and does not speak the truth, they have taught their tongue to speak lies [*mentored by the false-father as opportunists*]; they **weary themselves committing iniquity** [*in Worthless' labor-camp*]. ⁶**Your dwelling is in the midst of deceit** [*"refuge of lies" Isa. 28:17*]; **through deceit** [*DNA corrupted by the lie*] **they refuse to know Me** [*suppress, deny, and disown the true Triune-God*]," declares the Lord (Jer. 9:3-6).

As Jeremiah's *true* Father, God *purged* the corrupt desires and rationale of the false-father out of him and diligently *mentored* him in kingdom economics as a steward-son:

² Crabs are kept together in a bucket without a lid knowing that none will escape because as soon as one tries to climb out of the bucket, the others grab it and pull it back down.

18:15For My people have **forgotten Me** [*in self-absorption*], they burn incense to **worthless** gods [*cherished mediums of self-worth-ship*] and they have **stumbled** from their ways, from the **ancient paths** [*downward ascent into God Most High*], to walk in **bypaths** [*mirages of the false-father*], not on a **highway** [*the Way of Christ who practiced kingdom economics as a Man*]. 15:19...If you **return** [*exchange the lie for the truth*], then I will **restore** [*re-gene-rate*] you—before Me you will stand; and if you **extract the precious from the worthless**, you will become My spokesman [*mature steward-son and ambassador of God Most High*]. They [*opportunists*] for their part may turn to you, but as for you, you must not turn to them [*participate in their corruption and con-fusion*] (Jer. 18:15; 15:19).

The word "extract" implies **mixture**. As immature, "**double-minded**" believers (see James 1:8; 4:8), we suffer *the torment of choice*—a mixture that makes us precariously vulnerable to Worthless' schemes. There is *mixture* in our affections: a love for God but at the same time **a love of self in its natural habitat**—*me* in my familiar world. John warned, "If anyone **loves the world** [*desiring desire in Worthless' economy*] and the things of the world [*opportunities for self-indulgence*], the **Agape** [*fuse-able DNA*] of the Father is not in him" (1 John 2:15). Paul observed that there is a *mixture* of natures within us half-formed children of God: "For the flesh [*naturalized in eros, the lie*] sets its **desire** against the Spirit [*of Truth, Agape, gene-rosity*], and the Spirit against the flesh; for these are in opposition to one another, so that **you may not do the things that you please** [*desiring desire: self-indulgence, self-will, self-worth-ship*]" (Gal. 5:17).

A *double-minded* believer suffers the *torment* of constant magnetism to deadly, hook-laden lures—counterfeits shrewdly customized by Worthless to keep each unique individual **caught in a partial eclipse** from the Light of the *knowledge* of the glory. Truly, the most miserable existence possible is a particular form of knowing: to *know* about the Light and *know* you belong in the Light but also *know* you are **snared in the darkness by your own insatiable desire**, which you *know* is impossible to satisfy. You are leashed by your own self-will to the accuser who delights in condemning you day and night! Though it would have been easier *not* to *know* and though you have many times exhausted yourself trying to **suppress** *knowing* in self-deception, it's simply too late, you already *know*!

God Most High *exalted* **Solomon** and made him "wiser than all men" (1 Kings 4:31). Yet, it seems the false-father was *shrewder* in *eros* rationale since he effectively moved Solomon to buy into his lie, **sell his inheritance**, and live out his remaining days in an **ever-broadening eclipse**. For the purpose of remaining sober and alert in the fear of the Lord, we should try to understand how Solomon plummeted in upward descent so we can learn to discern Worthless' custom-designed schemes. Before Solomon fell, he wrote: "**A man who wanders** [*in eros, fission*] **from the way of understanding** [*"the Way" of Triune-Agape*] **will rest in the assembly of the dead** [*the living dead: fruitless, barren, zombies, existing in an eclipse*]" (Prov. 21:16). Using the gift of wisdom that God granted him, Solomon saw into the incorruptible God but simultaneously peered into the weakness of his own corrupt, *fallen* nature—*desiring desire*:

> [23]I tested all this with wisdom, and I said, "I will be wise," but it was **far from me**. [24]What has been [*spiritual reality of God Most High*] is **remote** and exceedingly **mysterious** [*eclipsed*]. Who can discover it? [25]I directed my mind to know, to investigate and to seek wisdom and an explanation, and to know **the evil of folly** [*self-indulgence, self-will, self-worth-ship*] and the **foolishness of madness** [*eros rationale*]. [26]And I discovered more bitter than death **the woman whose heart is snares and nets**, whose hands are chains [*daughter/agent of the false-father Worthless*]. One who is pleasing to God [*reciprocates His Self-forsaking Love*] will **escape** from

her, but the sinner [*tyrannized by desiring desire*] will be **captured** by her (Eccl. 7:23-26).

Curiously, it was these very snares, nets, and chains that **dragged Solomon down into faithlessness and fission from the Most High**. Though he was aware of Satan's devices, this ancient opportunist shrewdly exploited the king's insatiable desire for two related things: **women** *and* building an **empire of dirt** by entering into marriage alliances with foreign nations. Taking girls in marriage for political advantage is buying and selling human beings in Worthless' marketplace. When Solomon **con-fused** himself to the daughters of foreign kings, he did not realize they were actually Worthless' own daughters mentored as shrewd opportunists and that they came as a package deal complete with foreign gods. "Solomon **held fast** to these in love [*con-fusion in eros*]…and his wives turned his heart away after other gods" (1 Kings 11:2-4). In self-exaltation and inebriated by *desiring desire*, **Solomon overestimated himself** as the wisest man and *bought into* his own lie that he could easily influence these submissive women into the ways of the God of Israel; however, they led him as *their* submissive captive into a total eclipse.

Before Solomon *fell*, he had written: "The **way** of the wicked [*desiring desire, buying and selling one another*] is like **darkness** [*fission, eclipse*]; they do not know over what they **stumble**" (Prov. 4:19). Paul made plain that the foremost objective of the false-father is perpetuating and *broadening* this eclipse:

> [3]And even if our gospel is **veiled** [*eclipsed in secret mystery*], it is veiled to those who are **perishing** [*in eros, individualism, con-fusion, fission*], [4]in whose case **the god of this world** [*fallen one; the father of the lie*] **has blinded the minds of the unbelieving** [*dispirited dirt-bags, truth-suppressors*] so that they might not see the **light** of the gospel of the **glory of Christ** [*invitation to be fused into the God-Man Nucleus*], who is the image of God [*Most High*].... [6]For God, who said, "Light shall shine out of darkness," [*in the natural creation*] is the One [*Trinity in fusion*] who has shone in our hearts to give the **Light** of the **knowledge** of the **glory of God** [*fusion Oneness in mutual exaltation, perichoresis*] **in the face of Christ** [*the God-Man Nucleus*] (2 Cor. 4:3-6).

The secular world is certainly eclipsed from God Most High as many of us judgmental Christians often point out, but do we half-inebriated, self-righteous believers recognize that we ourselves still live in a partial eclipse? Can we acknowledge we are still dirt-bags who act upon the compulsions of insatiable desire and participate in Worthless' economy? Though we are not enemies of Christ, we as believers can be "enemies of the cross of Christ" (Phil. 3:18). We can regard with indifference and suspicion the very instrument God sacrificially provided to break the power of our insatiable desire on a "daily" basis (Luke 9:23) and progressively de-fuse our con-fusion to Worthless. Paul testified that through the cross, "the world has been crucified to me, and I to the world" (Gal. 6:14). Paul also urged believers: "Do not be partakers with the sons of disobedience [*con-fusion with opportunists in Worthless' marketplace*]; for you were formerly darkness [*creatures of the eclipse*], but now you are Light in the Lord; walk as **children of Light [remain fused together in the Nucleus by practicing kingdom economics]**" (Eph. 5:8).

As our Shepherd, Jesus sees us wayward sheep as we cannot see ourselves; He knows when we have wandered back into Worthless' marketplace. He knows long before we do when we have *fallen* into an eclipse:

> [4]I have this against you, that you have **left your first love** [*lit. the Agape you had for one another at the first; e.g. allowed relational fission to enter in among you*]. [5]Therefore remember from where you have **fallen** [*out of God Most High*], and repent and do the deeds you did at first [*practice kingdom economics: sacrificial self-giving*]; or else I [*the Nucleus of Triune-Jealous*] am coming to you and will **remove your lampstand**

[*earthen vessels intended to manifest Triune-Light by **relational fusion***] out of its place unless you **repent** [*return to the economy of the kingdom*] (Rev. 2:4-5).

Apart from the fusion glory of God in Christ dwelling within our lampstand, we are nothing more than dispirited dirt-bags filled with Worthless' ashes! As the foremost economic Advisor, Jesus intentionally used *economic terms* to confront the **double-minded believers in His own church** in the city of Laodicea who were *captivated* by mammon, *participating* in Worthless' marketplace, and *existing* in an **eclipse**:

[17]You say, "**I am rich** [*in Worthless' world*], and have become **wealthy** [*cherishing counterfeits as true treasure*], and have need of nothing [*self-sufficient*]," and **you do not know** that you are wretched, and miserable and **poor** and blind and naked [*individualists who keep buying into the false-father and sustaining abuse in his custody*], [18]**I advise you to buy from Me gold refined by fire** [*My own sacrificial self-giving DNA tested and proven fuse-able through the cross*] so that you may **become rich** [*with genuine treasure: ability to participate in the economy of God Most High*], and **white garments** so that you may **clothe yourself** [*in My own righteousness: a life-giving spirit*], and that

the shame of your nakedness may not be revealed [*exposed as a worthless taker/ opportunist*]; and **eye salve** to anoint your eyes so that you may **see** [*discern genuine from counterfeit; extract precious from worthless*] (Rev. 3:17-18).

Twelve Stages of Relational Fission

The narratives and teachings of the Bible make it clear that we individualists exist "in darkness"— **eclipsed** from the Triune-Most High—because we "**sell**" and "**exchange**" God and one another *for personal gain*. Our minor, day-to-day transactions lead us to make *major* ones. This *process* of relational fission begins very subtly and leads to **relational disasters**, which each and every one of us has suffered both as a *victim* and as an *offender*. If we can understand, practically, **how fission progresses** *within* us and *between* us, we can sober up, recognize when it is happening in our daily lives, and choose to relate to one another in a more excellent, *Trinity-like* way— *downward ascent*.

The corruptible seed (see 1 Pet. 1:23) or heredity of *eros* individual-ism, which each one of us was born with, not only causes one's own de-gene-ration but also the deterioration and decay of his relationship to God and other human beings. As an agent of fission, the false-father Worthless sowed this seed of corruption (see Matt. 13:28); as an unclean spirit, he breathes upon this seed within us; and as an opportunist, he instigates relational faithlessness, fission, and destruction among us. All twenty-seven books of the New Testament expose and confront this dynamic of relational fission using words such as "enmities, strife, **jealousy**, outbursts of anger, disputes, dissensions, factions, envying" (Gal. 5:20). James identified this unholy seed as "bitter jealousy and selfish ambition" (James 3:14-16). According to Matthew, "Pontius Pilate knew that **because of envy** the Jews had handed Jesus over" (Matt. 27:18). In order to recognize the strategy of our shrewd enemy and effectively discern and thwart his schemes and opportunities to divide us, we must understand how this unholy seed germinates, awakens, and matures. "He who separates himself [*relational fission*] seeks his own desire [*eros individualism, desiring desire*]" (Prov. 18:1). Meditate on these twelve stages of relational fission:

DISTANCE→DEVALUE→DISASSOCIATE→DESERT→
DENY→ DEMEAN→ DISOWN→ DISINHERIT→
DEFECT→DEHUMANIZE→DESTROY→DEATH

Distance. A seed of relational decay first gains entry into a tiny hair-line fissure in the rock of our relational solidarity when we allow **distance** to subtly come between us, when we are not careful to sacrificially cleave to one another, and/or when we fail to "maintain the same *Agape*" (Phil. 2:2). When we begin to experience distance, we might say, "We are not quite as close as we used to be."

Devalue. This distance leads to devaluing you. I no longer cherish you as I once did; you are not as important in my life, and I naturally begin to think less of you. The upward descent or falling out has begun.

Disassociate. As I begin building a case against you I begin isolating and detaching myself from you. The more I withdraw or separate from you relationally, the stronger my case looks.

Desert. Soon, I begin calculating how you are a liability and an encumbrance to the attainment of my own desire, and when circumstances press, I review the case I have built against you and find it much easier to justify deserting you. Paul wrote to the Galatian church, "I am amazed that you are so quickly deserting Him who called you by the grace of Christ" (Gal. 1:6).

Deny. Now that I am no longer with you, I am unwilling to pay the cost of our previous association; therefore, I deny you. Jesus said to Peter, "This very night, before a rooster crows, you will deny Me three times" (Matt. 26:34).

Demean. Denying you before others soon leads me to demean you in the presence of others—rehearsing my list of complaints and indictments against you.

Disown. After the list is long enough, I am lead to publicly disown. After Peter was restored and filled with the Spirit, he confronted his countrymen:

¹³The God of our fathers has glorified His servant Jesus, the one whom you delivered [*betrayed*] and **disowned** in the presence of Pilate, when he had decided to release Him. ¹⁴But you **disowned** the Holy and Righteous One [*God-Man Nucleus*] and asked for a murderer to be granted to you [*in exchange*], ¹⁵but put to **death** the Prince of Life (Acts 3:13-15).

Disinherit. After disowning you, I can easily justify preventing you from becoming an heir. This is essentially **selling** a human being, yet unknowingly, we have sold *ourselves* and **fallen headlong into the momentum of Worthless' fission power**.

Defect. Soon, we are magnetized to and find a new and exciting *kinship* with those persons who envy and hate the person we are disinheriting. I *sell* the allegiance we once had between us and defect to your enemies.

Dehumanize. Once I've defected to your enemies I must justify my actions by depriving you of human qualities. Seeing you as an animal makes it easier to seek to destroy you. I have become an unwitting pawn and agent of Worthless' agenda to dehumanize you.

Destroy. Dehumanizing you, of course, makes it easier to destroy you, tear you to shreds, and bring you to ruin.

> The scribes and the Pharisees brought **a woman caught in adultery**, and having

set her in the center of the court, they said to Him, "Teacher, this woman has been caught in adultery, **in the very act**. Now in the Law Moses commanded us to **stone such women**; what then do You say?" They were saying this, testing Him, so that they might have grounds for accusing Him. But Jesus stooped down and with His finger wrote on the ground. But when they persisted in asking Him, He straightened up, and said to them, "He who is without sin among you, let him be the **first to throw a stone at her**." (John 8:3-7).

Death. After I have brought you to ruin and destroyed you, I begin looking for an opportunity for the physical action of your demise. "For out of the heart comes evil thoughts, **murders**..." (Matt. 15:19).

Consider how Joseph suffered all twelve stages of relational fission at the hands of his envious brothers; not only did they *demean* and *disown* him but they also sought his *death* saying, "Now then, come let us **kill** him, and throw him into one of the pits..." (Gen. 37:20). Yet, Joseph overcame these predatory opportunists by radical *Agape—giving* and *forgiving*. Joseph redeemed them from Worthless' nature and power and reconciled with them **by extreme self-forsaking Love**. Paul understood the power of *forgive-ness*:

[10]But one whom you forgive anything, I forgive also; for indeed what **I have forgiven**...I did it for your sakes in the presence of Christ, [11]**so that no advantage** would be taken of us by Satan [*the opportunist; agent of fission*], for we are not ignorant of his schemes [*relational fission*] (2 Cor. 2:10-11).

In each of his letters, Paul cites relationships that have *de-gene-rated* into fission; "Demas, having loved this present world [*self in its natural habitat*], has **deserted** me" (2 Tim. 4:10). From experience, Paul warned Timothy to recognize how this process occurs within ones we love:

[1]But realize this, that in the last days, difficult times will come [*the war will intensify*]. [2]For men will become **lovers of self** [*self worth-ship*], **lovers of money** [*mammon*], boastful, **arrogant** [*moving in upward descent*], revilers, disobedient to parents [*resent authority*], **ungrateful** [*gene-rosity received does not factor into their calculation*], unholy, [3]**unloving, irreconcilable** [*lodged in fission*], malicious gossips [*agents of fission*], **without self-control** [*tyrannized by instinctual compulsions of self-indulgence*], **brutal, haters of good**, [4]**treacherous, reckless** [*predators who capriciously destroy*

those who have loved them], conceited [*inebriated by self-absorption*], lovers of pleasure [*eros*] rather than lovers of God [*Agape*], **⁵holding to a form of godliness** [*apparent believers*] although they have **denied its power** [*fusion in Agape*]; Avoid such men as these. ⁶For among them are those [*religious opportunists*] who enter into households and **captivate** weak [*lit. idle*] women weighed down with sins [*dispirited dirt-bags; easy prey*], led on by various impulses. (2 Tim. 3:1-6).

The incorruptible seed of the perfected Man, Jesus, which the Spirit plants and matures within us, causes us to "**draw near**" (Heb. 4:16, 7:19; James 4:8) and "**join ourselves**" (1 Cor. 6:17) to the Lord and one another in sacrificial self-giving. Water baptism is an act of *relational fusion*—a public **identification** with Christ and His one many-membered body. Regardless of the price I must pay among those who disapprove, I claim association with Him before God, Satan, angels, and human beings. *Relationally*, the seed of *Agape* "**never fails**" (1 Cor. 13:8). Paul wrote, "O Corinthians, our heart is opened wide. You are not restrained by us, but you are **restrained in your own affections** [*self-love eclipses true love*]. Now in like **exchange** [*reciprocal gene-rosity*]—I speak as to children—open wide to us also" (2 Cor. 6:11-13). Paul addressed *relational fission* as a critical issue in each of his epistles. In Romans he warned:

[17]...keep your eye on those [*agents of Worthless, opportunists*] who cause **dissentions** [*fission*] and hindrances [*lit. occasions of stumbling*] contrary to the teaching [*fusion in Agape*] which you learned, and turn away from them. [18]For such men are **slaves**, not of the Lord Christ, but **of their own appetites** [*desiring desire*]; and by their smooth and flattering speech [*Agape with hypocrisy– the lie*] they deceive the hearts of the unsuspecting. [19]...be **wise** in what is good [*mentored in kingdom economics as sons of the Triune-Most High*] and **innocent** in what is evil [*individualism: Worthless' nature and economy*]. [20]**The God of peace** [*Three in fusion Oneness, perichoresis*] **will soon crush Satan** [*the instigator of fission*] **under your feet** (Rom. 16:17-20).

The most vivid illustration in the Scriptures of the process of relational fission, and Satan's full participation in it, is **Judas' betrayal of Jesus**. In a sense, Judas Iscariot uniquely represented each of us in whom the fission power of individualism [*upward descent*] is at work, the sum total of that served as the impetus of Jesus' betrayal. Further, it is clear that the influence of Worthless' economy and **the power of mammon** were the primary forces that led Judas to *defect* to the false-father and *devalue, disown,* and *destroy* Jesus.

"When the devil had finished every temptation, he left Jesus until an **opportune time**" (Luke 4:13). As a shrewd opportunist, Worthless watched, waited, and found occasion against Jesus by *luring* one of His twelve disciples and gaining a foothold in him through the **medium of mammon**. Judas "was a **thief**, and as he had the money box, he used to **pilfer** what was put into it" (John 12:6). From the time he began embezzling up to the day the seed of the idea to betray Jesus entered into him, Judas incrementally *sold himself* into Worthless' power by practicing and *maturing* in **corruption**; therefore, as an unwitting apprentice, he was **mentored by the false-father as an opportunist**:

> [14]Then one of the twelve, named Judas Iscariot, went to the chief priests [*defected to Jesus' enemies*] [15]and said, "What are you willing to **give me** to betray Him to you?" And they weighed out **thirty pieces of silver** to him. [16]From then on he began looking for a good **opportunity** to betray Jesus (Matt. 26:14-16).

Though Judas' betrayal was premeditated, it is no coincidence that his scheme was irreversibly launched during **the Last Supper,** which Jesus *shared* with His disciples. As the Nucleus of the Triune-God, Jesus was preparing to comprehensively sacrifice Himself body and soul and spirit. The bread of Christ's body is three Ingredients mixed and baked by *Agape* into One Cake; the wine of His blood is the divine nature made communicable to human beings in a new, incorruptible bloodline—fuse-able DNA. The bread of His body and the wine of His blood, which Jesus freely gave them to eat and drink represent the **currency** of the economy of the kingdom—the **sacrificial Self-giving** of the Triune-God that enables us to reciprocate in *gene-rosity* to Them. The thirty pieces of silver represent **mammon**, the currency of the world economy—the power of *desiring desire* and the means to chase the mirage of **self-indulgence** in Worthless' world. Jesus said:

> [18] …"He who eats My bread has lifted up his **heel** against Me [*stands on Me in the crab bucket in self-exaltation*]." [21]…Jesus… became troubled in spirit, and testified and said, "Truly, truly, I say to you, that one of you will **betray** Me." [22]The disciples began looking at one another, at a loss to know of which one He was speaking.… [26]Jesus then answered, "That is the one for whom I shall **dip the morsel and give it to him** [*a full share in the One Cake of the kingdom*]." … [27]After the **morsel** [*receiving and "eating Jesus" in hypocrisy*], **Satan then entered into him.** Therefore Jesus said to him, "What you do, do quickly." [30]… So after receiving the morsel **he went out**

immediately [*in the power of fission*]; and it was **night** [*full eclipse*] (John 13:18-30).

Kiss of Betrayal

The predatory nature of the false-father had come to full maturity in Judas; therefore, Jesus' extravagant, relational *gene-rosity* only served to inflame Judas' "envious eye" (see Matt. 20:15). The intimate manner of Judas' betrayal—"a **kiss**"—made evident that he transacted an "**exchange**" according to the principles of Worthless' economy: he intentionally **sold** the "unfathomable riches" of *reciprocal gene-rosity* with God in Christ in order to **invest himself** into mammon. "Judas approached Jesus to **kiss** Him [*sign of relational solidarity in Agape*]. But Jesus said to him, 'Judas, are you **betraying** the Son of Man **with a kiss** [*Agape with hypocrisy*]?'" (Luke 22:48). Matthew recorded it this way:

> [48]Now he who was betraying Him gave them [*Jesus' enemies*] a **sign**, saying, "Whomever I **kiss**, He is **the one** [*e.g. God's choice Cornerstone/Nucleus sent to displace "me"*], **seize Him**." [49]Immediately Judas went to Jesus and said, "Hail Rabbi!" and **kissed Him**. [50]And Jesus said to him, "Friend, do what you have come for" (Matt. 26:48-50).

The kiss of betrayal may be compared to a present-day thermo-nuclear bomb. This bomb actually consists of two bombs in one casing: an atomic bomb in which atoms of plutonium are split (fission) and a hydrogen bomb in which atoms of hydrogen fuse. First, the fission bomb detonates in order to produce the heat required for the hydrogen atoms in the second, more powerful bomb to fuse, detonate, and yield an *exponential* explosion. The kiss of betrayal was **a fusion bomb** with a **fission detonator** devised by the father of the lie as a weapon of mass destruction.

Worthless' bomb, which Judas carried upon his lips, contained within it the full fission power of *all* our relational hypocrisy, treachery, and defection that effectively blew the Nucleus of the Trinity apart. Yet, Jesus willingly and intentionally embraced this **lethal kiss**. Because Satan is a *self-deceived* deceiver, he believed *himself* to be the sole choreographer of these events. Yet, above and beyond his shrewd, calculative scheme, there existed the eternal, **redemptive plan** of God Most High. *Before* Lucifer (aka Worthless) existed, the *eternal* Father, Son, and Spirit purposed to demonstrate Their extreme **Self-forsaking Love** by making human beings sharers in it.

Relational, inter-personal **fusion** is not possible without *free* individuals. *First* our Triune-Creator granted each human being **freedom** knowing we would *abuse* that freedom in self-worth-ship and ultimately sell, disown, and **betray** Them. *Then*, Father, Son, and Spirit intentionally *embraced* our kiss of betrayal, exhausting into the midst of *Themselves and* into the Nucleus of Their own, eternal Oneness the entirety of the power of *our* relational fission: "My God [*Father*], My God [*Spirit*], why have You **forsaken** Me [*the Son*]?" (Matt. 27:46). To truly set us *corrupt* individualists free to participate in the *incorruptible* economy of the kingdom as sons and daughters, the Triune-Most High had to **conquer corruption itself**—the *abuse* of freedom, double-mindedness, the torment of choice, and opportunism. "…now once at the consummation of the ages He [*the Son and Nucleus of God Most High*] has been manifested to **put away sin** [*corruption, self-worth-ship, upward descent*] **by the sacrifice of Himself** [*downward ascent*]" (Heb. 9:26).

Exchanged for Silver

Centuries before Christ came into Worthless' world, the prophet Zechariah foretold that He would be **exchanged** for "thirty pieces of silver." Zechariah wrote:

> [4]Thus says the Lord my God [*my Nucleus*], "Pasture the flock doomed to **slaughter** [*God's people invested in Worthless' economy*]. [5]**Those who buy them** [*the dispirited people of God*] **slay them** and go unpunished, and each of those who **sell them** says, 'Blessed be the Lord, for I have become **rich!**' And their own

shepherds have no pity on them [*devoid of Agape*]. ⁶...but, behold, I will cause the men [*predatory opportunists*] to fall, each into another's power...." ⁷So I pastured the flock doomed to slaughter, hence the **afflicted** [*wretched, thrown down*] of the flock. And I took for myself two staffs: the one I called **Favor** [*Agape*], and the other I called **Union** [*Fusion*]....

⁸**Then I annihilated** the three shepherds [*predators*] in one month, for my soul was impatient with them, and their soul also was weary of [*lit. detested*] me. ⁹Then I said, "**I will not pasture** [*lit. give to*] you. What is to die, let it die, and what is to be annihilated, let it be annihilated; and let those who are left eat one another's flesh [*bite, devour, consume one another Gal. 5:1*]." ¹⁰**I took my staff Favor** [*Agape*] **and cut it in pieces** [*fission*], to break my covenant which I had made with all the peoples....

¹²I said to them, "If it is good in your sight, **give me my wages;** but if not, never mind!' So they weighed out **thirty shekels of silver** as my wages. ¹³Then the Lord said to me, "Throw it to the potter,

that magnificent price at which I was valued [*devalued, disowned, disinherited*] **by them**." So I took the thirty shekels of silver and threw them to the potter in the house of the Lord. [14]**Then I cut in pieces my second staff Union** [*fusion*], to break the brotherhood between Judah and Israel (Zech. 11:4-14).

Only the fusion power released in the sacrificial Self-giving of God in Christ could redeem us dirt-bags from the fission power and eclipse of Worthless' corrupt nature and economy.

Jesus, Son of the Most High God

Into the midst of the relational *fission, eclipse,* and *famine* of Worthless' world, "Jesus, Son of the Most High God" (Luke 1:32; Mark 5:7) entered and lived among the *de-gene-rate* **captives** of its *eros*-driven economy: dispirited dirt-bags corrupted from the inside out with the lie, individualists tyrannized by *desiring desire*, opportunists **who sit in the marketplace and call to one another** (see Matt. 11:16). At the time John the Baptist was born, his father Zacharias prophesied of the imminent arrival of God in Christ:

> [78]Because of the tender mercy [*superabundant gene-rosity*] of our God, with which the **Sunrise from on high**

[*Nucleus of the Triune-Most High*] **will visit us** [*suffering in our self-precipitated famine*], [79]**to shine** [*Life-producing Light: photosynthesis*] **upon those who sit in darkness** [*the eclipse of Worthless' world economy: upward descent*] **and the shadow of death** [*con-fusion, fission decay*], to guide our feet into **the way of peace** [*the bountiful economy of the kingdom: downward ascent*] (Luke 1:78-79).

As the human Nucleus of the fusion of the Triune-God, Jesus entered as "the Light of the world" (John 8:12) and began *engaging* the inebriated individualists by living, teaching, embodying, and imparting the way of God Most High. As a first-hand witness, Peter declared, "God raised up His **Servant** and sent Him [*as a Man*] **to bless you** [*dispirited dirt-bags*] **by turning every one of you** [*corrupt individualists*] **from your wicked ways** [*desiring desire, self-worth-ship, opportunism*]" (Acts 3:26). Jesus, Son of the Most High God, came as a Man on the earth **to bring the economy of the kingdom, in Himself, down to us**: "For you know the grace [*sacrificial Self-giving*] of our Lord Jesus Christ, that though He was **rich** [*Son of God: first-hand participant in the fullness of the Triune-Dwelling Place*], yet for your sake He became **poor** [*emptied Himself to become the Son of Man, our Advocate*], so that you through His **poverty** [*comprehensive Self-expenditure*] might become **rich**" (2 Cor. 8:9).

The archangel Gabriel was sent to a lowly virgin living in a small, insignificant village, to announce the manner of His coming:

> [31]And behold, you will conceive in your womb and bear a son, and you shall name Him Jesus. [32]He will be **great** and will be called the **Son of the Most High**; and the Lord God will give Him the throne of His father David; [33]…and His kingdom will have no end. [35]…The Holy Spirit will come upon you, and the [*fusion*] **power of the Most High** will overshadow you; and for that reason the **holy** [*eros-free*] **Child** shall be called the Son of God (Luke 1:31-35).

Curiously, the Son of the Most High—a Man destined to "be **great**"—entered a world of predators as a vulnerable infant born into very **humble** circumstances. He emerged from the womb in a **barn** and was wrapped and laid in a **feeding trough**; He was given as "the **true bread** out of heaven" (John 6:32) to be *broken* through crucifixion and distributed as "food" for beasts: "Behold the **Lamb of God** who takes away [*pays for with His own flesh and blood*] the sins of the world!" (John 1:29). From the start, God's idea of **greatness**—extreme Self-forsaking Love without hypocrisy or pretension—was altogether foreign and absurd in the economy of Worthless' world. The law and culture of the marketplace is **the**

survival of the fittest; entrepreneurial tyrants and shrewd opportunists may be resented and hated by those whom they have defrauded and exploited, but they are secretly *admired* and *esteemed* among the wolf-pack for enlarging themselves by **devouring** others. Who, then, would *worth-ship* a God Who gives Himself as **food**?

Charles Spurgeon observed that the Highest stooped to become the lowest and the greatest took His place among the least. Who in Worthless' world could even imagine a *downward ascent*? The announcement of the birth of the Son of God did not come to the high priest at the temple in Jerusalem, nor to King Herod, nor to Caesar, nor to any **power-broker** in any secular or religious epicenter as everyone would have expected. Rather, the Triune-Most High chose to celebrate the incarnation of Their Nucleus with ordinary shepherds in a remote area with a handful of blue-collar night-shift workers considered nobodies in the marketplace:

> [8]...there were some shepherds staying out in the fields and keeping watch over their flocks by night. [9]And an angel of the Lord suddenly stood before them, and the **glory of the Lord** [*fusion yield of Triune-Agape*] shone around them.... [13]And suddenly there appeared with the angel a multitude of the heavenly host praising God and saying, [14]"**Glory to God in the highest**

[*Triune-Most High*], **and on earth peace** [*the economy of Their shared kingdom*] **among men**…" (Luke 2:8, 13-14).

The true, Self-emptying Love, which Father, Son, and Spirit *are* as Individuals and *share* as One, moved God Most High to **descend** in humility and fullness to **arrogant** mankind—first in the Person of the Son, Jesus, and then in the Person of His Spirit, reaching to us in compassion and *gene-rosity* even while we sit eclipsed and imprisoned in the delusional darkness and misery of our own **self-exaltation** and famine. Father gene-rously feeds beasts! Jesus said: "For **the bread of God** [*fullness of the Triune-Most High*] is that which **comes down** out of heaven [*three Ingredients mixed and baked by Agape into One Cake: a flesh and blood Man*], and **gives life** to the world.…**I AM** the bread of life; **he who comes to Me** [*e.g. reciprocates God's Love by losing his life into the God-Man Nucleus*] **will not hunger** [*suffer famine*]…" (John 6:33-35).

The circumstances of Christ's birth as well as the manner of His life, death, and resurrection were wholly without the attention-seeking, publicity, pretense, or promotional embellishments to be expected in the economy of Worthless' world. The life and ways of Jesus are "the exact representation" (Heb. 1:3) of the **unpretentious** quality of the glory and greatness of God Most High—three, **humble** Individuals who exalt and add to One Another. In the Person of Christ, the Triune-God feed *Themselves* to us, both to satisfy our hunger and as a means of administering an **Antidote** able to *re-gene-rate* incurable individualists, addicts of insatiable desires, and predatory opportunists. "The Son of Father's *Agape*" (Col. 1:13) brought down to the earth, in Himself, the economy of heaven:

> [27]A man can **receive** nothing [*true, genuine, of worth*] unless it has been **given** him from heaven [*God Most High*].... [31]**He who comes from above** [*Jesus, Son of the Most High*] **is above all,** he who is of the earth [*dispirited dirt-bag*] is from the earth [*born de-gene-rate*] and speaks of the earth [*cherishes dirt: material things and self in its natural habitat*]. He who comes from heaven is above all [*panoramic, bird's-eye view of the kingdom and the world*]. [32]**What He has seen and heard** [*as an eternal participant in Triune-Agape, reciprocal gene-rosity, fusion glory*], **of that He testifies**; and no one receives His testimony [*eclipsed by self-focus and individualism*]. [33]He who has received His testimony [*e.g. how the economy of the kingdom works*] has set his seal to this, that **God is true** [*Three relationally faithful to One Another and to Their faithless creation*] (John 3:27-33).

The Son of God came on the earth as our "**Forerunner**" (Heb. 6:20) to practice participating in the economy of the kingdom of heaven *as a Man* and to guide us into the transcendent reality of God Most High.

> ⁵Have this attitude [*life-giving spirit*] in yourselves which was also in Christ Jesus, ⁶who, although He existed in the form of **God** [*One of the Three eternal Primaries*], did not consider equality with God [*Most High*] a thing to be **grasped** [*promoted or preserved in eros: upward descent*], ⁷but **emptied Himself**, taking on the form of a **bond-servant** [*sent to lift us into the Most High*].... ⁸Being found in appearance as a **man**, He **humbled Himself** by becoming obedient to the **point of death**, even death on a cross [*the most shameful, humiliating, cursed execution possible*]. ⁹For this reason also, **God highly exalted Him** [*downward ascent*], and bestowed on Him [*as a Man*] the name which is **above** every name [*the shared name of Triune-Most High*] (Phil. 2:5-9).

For the sake of us **corrupt** human beings, the Triune-God developed *within* the Man Jesus an **Antidote** containing three, active ingredients: *Themselves* dwelling in the relational fullness of reciprocal *gene-rosity*. In order to be effective, this *re-gene-rative* Antidote had to be the exact **incorruptible** likeness of the Triune-God—"the divine nature" (2 Pet. 1:4)—tested, perfected, and proven *within* a Man.

Lucifer and Adam *corrupted* themselves by self-worth-ship, but "the last Adam [*Jesus*] **became a life-giving spirit**" (1 Cor. 15:45). Lucifer and Adam *exalted* themselves and **fell** [*upward descent*], but the Man Jesus *humbled* Himself and **ascended** [*downward ascent*]because Father and Spirit **lifted** Him: "Jesus [*the tested perfected Man*] is the one whom God **exalted** to His right hand as a Prince and a Savior, **to grant repentance** [*embody and administer the Antidote*]…" (Acts 5:31). As a Man, the Son of God perfected this Antidote within Himself by willingly retaking and passing the **tests of self-denial** which Lucifer, Adam, and all his subsequent offspring failed. Jesus said, "Take courage, I have **overcome the world** [*Worthless' economy: self-worth-ship, desiring desire, mammon, opportunism*]" (John 16:33). He also said:

> [30]…the ruler of the world is coming [*false-father "Worthless" will try to prove Me a fraud, imposter, counterfeit*], and **he has nothing in Me** [*not a single point of DNA-match or con-fusion, e.g. I cannot be bought*]; [31]but so that the world [*dirt-bags, individualists*] may know that I **Agape** the Father [*gen-uine sacrificial Self-giving*], I do exactly as the Father commanded Me [*lit. Greek: as the Father does, so I do; e.g. I "seek first His"*] (John 14:30-31; see also John 10:17-18).

Over the thirty-three years Jesus lived on the earth, He *perfected* in Himself reciprocal gene-rosity with Father and Spirit and effectively **overcame Worthless** and his world; therefore, "all the fullness" (Col. 2:9) of the Triune-Most High and the economy of Their shared kingdom were *perfected* within Him as a Man—"**a Son, made perfect forever**" (Heb. 7:28). In daily life, the Son Jesus walked in this transcendent reality:

> [12]I am the **Light** of the world [T*riune-Spectrum in One Beam*]; he who follows Me [*"the Way" of sacrificial Self-giving*] will not walk in **darkness** [*individualism, fission, eclipse*], but will have the **Light of life** [*photosynthesis, fusion Oneness in reciprocal Agape*]. [14]...for I know **where I came from** [*eternal Son of God Most High*] and **where I am going** [*back into the fusion of the Trinity as a Man*]. [21]...I go away, and you will seek Me, and you will **die in your sin** [*self-worth-ship*]; where I am going, you [*the eros individualist*] cannot come.

> [23]...You are **from below** [*thrown down; dispirited dirt-bags*], I AM **from above** [*Man participating in the economy of God Most High*]; you are **of this world** [*sons of Worthless*], I am **not of this world**. [24]...for unless you believe that **I am He** [*Triune-*

God in fullness in Christ], you will die in your sins [*corruption, fission decay*]. [28]... When you **lift up** [*crucify*] the Son of Man, then you will know that **I am He, and I do nothing on My own initiative** [*autonomously*], but I speak these things as the Father **taught** Me [*learned as a Man*]. [29]And He who sent Me is with Me [*God and Man in fusion Oneness, perfected in unity*]; He has not left Me alone [*in fission*], for **I always do the things that are pleasing to Him** [*e.g. I perpetually yield heart, mind, will, and strength into Him*] (John 8:12-29).

Explaining to these men how they would crucify Him in envy and **self-preservation**, Jesus used the words "**lift up.**" According to *eros* rationale, this choice of words to describe being hung on a cross is incomprehensible and perplexing: "the word of the cross is foolishness to those who are perishing [*in self-worth-ship: upward descent*]" (1 Cor. 1:18). According to *Agape* rationale, however, "*lift up*" makes perfect sense: *downward ascent.* The crucifixion served as the **acid test**—the unmistakable and defining **proof**—that the Man Jesus was *not* of Worthless' world and that He was *perfected* in the **Self-forsaking** Love of God Most High; it is *impossible* for Father, Son, or Spirit, as Individuals or as One, to save Their own lives. The essential nature and fusion power of the

Persons of the Trinity is losing Themselves *into* One Another—*expending* Themselves *for* One Another and *for* us:

> [39]And those passing by were hurling abuse at Him, [40]…saying, "**save Yourself!** If You are the Son of God come down from the cross [*Self-preservation*]…. [42]He saved others; **He cannot save Himself**…. [43]… for He said, 'I am the Son of God'" (Matt. 27:39-42).

Three Burden Bearers

The Triune-God is Most High because each of the three Eternals exalt One Another and never Himself. The very bedrock of the fruit-bearing economy of the kingdom is that Father, Son, and Spirit are humble burden-bearers. According to the economic blueprints of the Triune-God, Paul urged us to, "Bear **one another's burdens**, and thereby fulfill the law of Christ [*the law of Triune-Agape*]" (Gal. 6:2). The gene-rative source of the productivity of the economy of the kingdom and the secret of its superabundant bounty is that the Persons of the Trinity Themselves are the work-force! This unimaginable mystery of God Most High was fully revealed in Christ. En route to the cross, Jesus purposefully entered Jerusalem on a "beast of burden" in fulfillment of His mandate to introduce us to this transcendent economy. Matthew recorded Jesus' triumphal entry into Jerusalem:

⁵Say to the daughter of Zion [*many-membered bride*], "Behold **your King** [*Triune-Groom–God in Christ*] is coming to you, gentle, and **mounted on a donkey**, even on a colt, the foal [*offspring*] of a **beast of burden**." ⁹…The crowds going ahead of Him and those who followed, were shouting, "Hosanna [*lit. "help," or "save I pray"*] to the Son of David; blessed is He who comes in the name of the Lord [*Nucleus of the Trinity*]; **Hosanna in the highest** [*salvation from God Most High; Three who exalt One Another lifting mankind into Themselves in Christ Jesus*]!" ¹²…And Jesus entered the temple [*Jealous-for Father and Spirit*] and drove out all those who were **buying and selling** [*practicing Worthless' economy*] in the temple… (Matt. 21:5-12).

To make His revelatory entrance into the city, Jesus did not mount Himself upon the stately, pure-bred steed worthy of an **earthly king**; rather, He requisitioned the colt of a donkey saying "The Lord has need of it" (Luke 19:31). The beast of burden represents the Trinity—**Three burden-bearers**—and the colt represents the Man Jesus Christ, an exact DNA-match of the humble Triune-God. "God was in Christ reconciling the world to Himself" (2 Cor. 5:19). As *burden-bearers*, the Triune-God purposed to lift mankind *out* of Worthless' world economy and *into* Themselves—*into* the economy of God Most High: "Bear one another's burdens, and thereby fulfill the law of Christ" (Gal. 6:2). God's way of **downward ascent** and reciprocal burden-bearing was altogether foreign to fallen human beings, even to the religious Jews who had memorized the Law and the Prophets, which clearly foretold He would come "humble, and mounted on a donkey, even on a colt, the foal of a donkey" (Zech. 9:9). Jesus warned His disciples:

> [2]The scribes and the Pharisees…[3]say things and do not do them [*Agape with hypocrisy, the lie*]. [4]**They tie up heavy burdens and lay them on men's shoulders**, but they themselves are **unwilling** to move them with so much as a finger. [5]But they do all their deeds to be noticed by men [*eros look good*].… [6]They love the **place of honor** at banquets and the chief seats in the synagogues [7]…and being called Rabbi by men [*Worthless' nature: pretense, self-exaltation*].

> [8]But do not be called Rabbi; for **One is your Teacher** [*our Mentor: Three burden-bearers in Self-giving Oneness*], **and you are all brothers** [*equality as fellow-heirs of one shared inheritance; burden-bearers working together as self-giving stewards of one shared*

estate]. [10]...Do not be called leaders; for **One is your leader**, that is, Christ [*God in Christ*]. [11]But **the greatest among you shall be your servant** [*kingdom economics*]. [12]Whoever **exalts himself** shall be humbled [*upward descent*]; and whoever **humbles himself** shall be exalted [*carried on the back of God in Christ into the Most High*] (Matt. 23:2-12).

In the humble, Self-giving manner of His life and in the comprehensive, Self-emptying manner of His death, the Man Jesus *embodied* and demonstrated the **burden-bearing Love** of the Triune-God:

[23]And **while being reviled**, He did not revile in return; while suffering, He uttered no threats, but kept entrusting Himself to Him [*the burden-bearer*] who judges righteously; [24]and He Himself **bore our** sins in His body on the cross, so that we might die to sin [*corruption in eros*] and live to righteousness [*incorruptible Agape*]; for by His wounds you were healed [*of desiring desire, individualism*] (1 Pet. 2:23-24).

He was perfected as a burden-bearer, a life-giving spirit Who comprehensively fulfilled God's eternal, redemptive purpose by humbling Himself to the point of death. "**God raised Him up** again [*into the Most High*], *putting an end to the agony of death* *[corruption, fission decay]*, since it was impossible for Him *[the all-true, fuse-able God-Man]* to be held in its *[fission]* power" (Acts 2:24). Isaiah gave us a precise understanding of the way God in Christ would break the power of death; the prophet foretold how God, as a Man, would Himself overcome the economy of Worthless' world that He might legally emancipate all of us dispirited dirt-bags whom the false-father has held captive in his labor-camp: "So it will be in that day *[Jesus' death and resurrection]*, that his burden *[the false-father's tyranny]* will be removed from your shoulders and his yoke from your neck, and the **yoke** *[of Worthless' nature and economy]* **will be broken** because of fatness *[e.g. a flesh and blood "Man" will outgrow the yoke]*" (Isa. 10:27). The Son Jesus willingly and sacrificially received into Himself, the fullness of the Trinity as well as all mankind; therefore, it was simply impossible for Worthless' yoke to fit on His human neck—it was "broken because of fatness"! As the seed of Christ matures in us individually and corporately, Worthless' yoke on our neck is also "broken because of fatness." Paul declared that the Man Jesus "was declared the Son of God *[Most High]* with *[fusion]* power by the resurrection **from the dead**, according to the Spirit of holiness *[certified eros-free by the witness of the Spirit]*, Jesus Christ our Lord" (Rom. 1:4). Paul also stated:

> [20]*[God]* **raised Him** *[the God-Man Nucleus]* from the dead and **seated Him**

[*and us in Him*] at His right hand **in the heavenly places** [*Son of Man, our Advocate, perfected in God Most High*], [21]**far above all rule and authority and power and dominion** [*Worthless' claim to the earth and all dispirited dirt-bags in it*].… [22]And He put all things in **subjection under His feet**, and gave Him as head over all things to the church, [23]which is His body [*many-membered bride made fit to cohabit with her Triune-Groom*], **the fullness of Him who fills all in all** [*with the superabundant bounty of reciprocal gene-rosity*] (Eph. 1:20-23).

Relational Fullness

The kingdom of God is best understood as an infinite progression of **relational fullnesses**: "There will be no end to the increase of His government or of peace" (Isa. 9:7). We enter and participate in these relational *fullnesses* according to **the measure of our faith:** *from faith to faith* and *from life to life* and *from glory to glory.* Faith means believing into, buying into, or relocating into these *fullnesses* of our Triune-God by **reciprocal faith-fullness**—practicing kingdom economics. Jesus called the Spirit "the Helper" (John 14:26); with the Spirit's help, we must see the kingdom and buy into its economy by practicing *reciprocal gene-rosity.* Through the eternal Spirit, David prophesied of

Jesus' ascension and what it would mean for us: "You [*the perfected, resurrected Man Jesus*] have **ascended on high**, You have led captive Your **captives** [*re-gene-rated human beings; "the Agape of Christ controls us" 2 Cor. 5:14*]; You have **received gifts among men** [*given birth to reciprocal self-givers*], even among the **rebellious** [*de-gene-rate individualists*] also, that the Lord God may **dwell** there [*cohabit with His children made new, fuse-able*]" (Ps. 68:18).

The Son of God Most High came to *lift* us dispirited dirt-bags out of Worthless' world economy, **mentor us in kingdom economics**, and *lift* us, in Himself, *into* His Own inheritance in God Most High. According to *Agape* rationale—**downward ascent**—Paul interpreted David's Psalm:

> [7]But to each one [*individual*] of us grace was given according to the measure of **Christ's gift** [*out from His infinite Person*]. [8]Therefore it says, "When He **ascended on high**, He led captive a host of **captives** [*e.g. Worthless' takers re-gene-rated into reciprocal self-givers*], and He gave gifts to men [*out of "the fullness" within Him*]." [9](Now this expression, "He **ascended**," what does it mean except that He also had **descended into the lower parts of the earth?** [*e.g. beneath the dirt, the realm of the dead: the inevitable destination of all corruptible men*]? [10]He who **descended** is

Himself also He who **ascended** [*with us in Him*] **far above all the heavens** [*e.g. above the created heavens into "the heaven of heavens"–God Most High*], so that He might **fill all things)** [*as sacrificial Self-sharers, the Trinity considered us to be a part of Their ultimate, relational fullness!*] (Eph. 4:7-10).

According to *the measure* we are willing to be led by the Spirit through the eclipse of our own self-focus and self-worth-ship, in that *measure* we are able to see Who the God-Man Jesus is—the Nucleus of the fusion of the Trinity and man—and we begin to enter and participate in the relational *fullnesses* of the kingdom *within* Him:

[9]But we do **see Him** [*Son of God Most High*] who was made for a little while **lower than the angels**, namely, Jesus, because of the suffering of death [*sacrificial Self-giving*] **crowned with glory and honor** [*a Man lifted into the Most High*], so that by the grace of God He might **taste death** [*the fall: corruption, fission*] **for everyone**. [10]**For it was fitting for** Him, for whom are all things [*Heir*], and through whom are all things [*combined and combining God-Man*], in **bringing many sons to glory** [*into His own inheritance in God Most High*], to perfect [*in the divine*

nature, *fuse-able DNA*] the author of their salvation through sufferings [*tests of self-denial and self-giving*]. **11For both He who** sanctifies and those who are sanctified are **all from one** Father [*genetic root: DNA-match in Agape*]; for which reason He is not ashamed to call them **brethren** [*one, fuse-able bloodline*] (Heb. 2:9-11).

Pioneering the Downward Ascent

It is estimated that over 90% of the inhabitants of earth acknowledge the existence of a God/Creator in one form or another, though some religions assert that god is essentially self, i.e. *God dwells within me as me.* Yet, the vast majority of human beings who believe in a god other than self, consider prayer to be like a long-distance, inter-galactic phone call to the Man upstairs[3] through some kind of outer-space satellite (i.e. Mary, a favorite saint, Muhammad, Buddha, Krishna, etc.)—a medium of communication that may or may not work but could be worth a try if the famine gets too severe! But there is a more excellent way:

---

[3] Scripture states that God is "on high" (Luke 1:78; Heb. 1:3). Because the three sacrificial Self-sharers are *all-true* to One Another in *Agape*; therefore, the Triune-God is "Most High." Father, Son, and Spirit **carry One Another up the stairs**; therefore, God is the Man upstairs. See *Plumbline, God Magnified, Part 6:* Appraising the Most High, Vol. 36.1 (2014) p. 7-11.

[14]Therefore, since we have a **great high priest** [*a Man*] who has passed through the heavens, Jesus the Son of God [*Most High*], let us hold fast our confession. [15]**For we do not have a high** priest [*worthless medium*] who cannot sympathize with our weaknesses [*desiring desire*], but One who has been tempted in all things [*in Worthless' marketplace*] as we are, yet **without sin** [*eros-free*]. [16]Therefore [*through this Overcomer dwelling within us*] let us draw near with confidence… (Heb. 4:14-16; see also 1 Tim. 2:5).

Jesus, Son of the Most High God, "emptied Himself, taking on the form of a bondservant" (Phil. 2:7); He was born in a barn; "He has **no stately form or** [*external*] **majesty** that we should **look upon** Him, **nor appearance** that we should be **attracted** to Him [*no pretentious allurement*]" (Isa. 53:2); He was devalued and betrayed for thirty pieces of silver, exchanged for a murderer, and crucified in weakness and "shame" (Heb. 12:2); but see this resurrected Man who *pioneered* the way of downward ascent for us as He is *now*:

[11]And I saw heaven opened, and behold, a white horse [*a King's steed*], and He [*the God-Man Nucleus*] who sat on it is called **Faithful and True,** and in righteousness [*Man tested and proven in Agape*] He

judges and wages war [*against the lie*]. [12]His eyes are a flame of fire [*consuming fire: fusion yield of the Trinity within Him*], and **on His head are many diadems** [*"all authority," Matt. 28:18*] [13]…and His name is called the Word of God [*Nucleus and Revealer of God Most High*].

[14]And the armies which are in heaven, clothed in fine linen [*the gift of His Own life-giving Spirit*], white and clean [*eros-free*] were **following Him** [*"the way, truth, and life," John 14:6*] on white horses. [15]From His mouth comes a **sharp sword** [*"two-edged" Heb. 4:12–perfected God-Man*], so that with it He may strike down the nations [*in corruption, con-fusion, counterfeit glory*], and He will rule them with a **rod of iron** [*e.g. Agape without hypocrisy or mixture: the non-negotiable Law of the kingdom*]; [16]…on His robe and on His thigh He has a name written, "**KING OF KINGS**, AND LORD OF LORDS" (Rev. 19:11-16).

Jesus presently wears "**many diadems**" upon His head because He *first* embraced the "**crown of thorns**" (John 19:5)—exhausting into Himself the curse of futility and famine. Through the Son Jesus, **God conquered the pinnacles** of all the governments, economies, corporations, and black-markets of all the nations in all ages. God also **handed over to this incorruptible God-Man all the authority and power** that accompany being king of the mountain, which corrupt men have vied for by buying and selling one another. "When God had disarmed the rulers and authorities, He made a public display of them, having **triumphed** over them through Christ" (Col. 2:15). The inhabitants of heaven extravagantly *worth-ship* this all-true King—God in Christ; in reciprocal generosity to Him, they "**cast their crowns before the throne**" (Rev. 4:10). Now, *this* Man Jesus is certainly qualified to teach you and me how to participate in the economy of the kingdom!

Kingdom Economics 101

By faith, we believers have *bought into* God in Christ; therefore, we have received the *incorruptible seed* and we are certainly "**born again** [*lit. born from above*]" (John 3:3). However, Christ is not yet fully formed [*re-gene-rated*] within us individually or corporately (see Gal. 4:19). The laws, culture, rationale, and economy of the kingdom of the Most High—*downward ascent*—still seem very **foreign** to us as half-formed children of God; we were **born first** into the eclipse of Worthless' world and have been deeply **acculturated** into his corrupt rationale and economy. Though most of us believers have not yet learned how to participate together in the economy of the kingdom, the Apostle John told us where to begin:

¹⁹We know that we are of God [*born from above: of the gen-uine, fuse-able seed of Triune-Agape*], and that the whole world [*an economic system*] lies in the power of the evil one [*"the father of the lie": eros*]. ²⁰And we know that **the Son of God** [*Most High*] **has come**, **and has given us understanding** [*of kingdom economics: reciprocal gene-rosity*] so that we may know Him who is true [*gen-uine, without hypocrisy*]; and we are **in Him** [*fused into the Triune-God*] who is true, **in His Son Jesus Christ** [*the God-Man Nucleus*]. This is the true God and **eternal life** [*the relational "fullness" of sharing one cohabitation: the kingdom*] (1 John 5:19-20).

The Son came as a Man to introduce us to the economy of heaven saying, "**My kingdom is not of this world**" (John 18:36). The kingdom of God in Christ is a relational, inter-Personal *infrastructure* built upon the fusion dynamic of *Agape*: true, sacrificial Self-giving Love. We have often reflected on Jesus' words, "Blessed are the **poor in spirit,** for theirs is the **kingdom** of heaven" (Matt. 5:3), but have we considered that this universal law *includes* Father, Son, and Spirit? It is the **Self-emptying humility** of each Individual of the Trinity toward One Another that yields the superabundant bounty of the kingdom and allows the fullness that They *share* to be the **inheritance** of each One—all for one and one for all!

In the economy of the world, individuals debit others to credit self; in the economy of the kingdom, individuals debit self to credit others. In the world, even the religious world, there is no such thing as a free gift; there is always a hook and a payoff. In the kingdom, "**freely you received, freely give** [*reciprocal gene-rosity*]" (Matt. 10:8). The economic system of Worthless' world is based in *the lie*—counterfeits of genuine treasure are crafted and marketed to appeal to the *insatiable desire* of individualists, to persuade them to believe they are getting something free and actually *buy into* it. The economy of the kingdom is founded upon *the truth*—"Buy truth, and do not sell it" (Prov. 23:23). Emigrating into the kingdom means **exchanging economies**:

> ⁴⁴The kingdom of heaven [*God Most High*] is like a **treasure** hidden in the field [*in the dirt*], which a man found and hid again [*seed of fuse-able DNA planted within*]; and from joy over it he goes and **sells all that he has** [*loses his life*] and **buys** that field. ⁴⁵**Again, the kingdom of heaven** is like a **merchant** seeking fine pearls, ⁴⁶**and upon finding one pearl of great value** [*fusion Oneness*], he went and **sold all** that he had and **bought** it (Matt. 13:44-46).

This economic parable provides us with a unique picture of **reciprocal gene-rosity** because the "man" who finds the kingdom and sacrificially *buys into* it can represent you or me, but it also describes the "Man" Jesus who **discovers us as dirt-bags hidden in the field**, *treasures* us, and buys the field. The many-membered "**bride**," which God treasures, is comprised of *redeemed* individualists who were once fixated upon acquiring and possessing the terra firma—we were all *buried* in the dirt! However, our **Triune-Groom** came in Christ "to **seek** and to save that which was lost [*e.g. fallen*]" (Luke 19:10).

Paul wrote, "God [*Father, Son, Spirit*] was in Christ reconciling the world [*His filthy, beloved bride*] to Himself" (2 Cor. 5:19). At the cross, our **Triune-Groom**, *sold all that He had* [*the Nucleus of the Trinity was torn in fission*] and *bought* the whole world so He could **lift His treasured bride out of the dirt!** *Reciprocal gene-rosity* means that we, His bride, demonstrate this *same* self-forsaking Love by *selling* our autonomous lives in the world [*self in its' natural habitat*] to *buy into* our Groom—the God-Man Nucleus of the Most High.

There is certainly economic success in Worthless' world, but no "great value [*true worth*]." Amassing earthly wealth is certainly possible, yet with mammon comes the **sorrow** of individualism—a famine of spirit and soul and body—where contentment and peace lie just out of reach. "It is the blessing of the Lord that makes rich, and He adds **no sorrow** to it" (Prov. 10:22). The economy of the kingdom operates according to the **law of *Agape***—sacrificial self-giving and self-sharing. Father, Son, and Spirit live according to this law. Individual human beings who understand and embrace the law of the Triune-God become *sharers* of Their rationale and economy of worth: they seek out and *treasure* one another, they become *rich* by reciprocal gene-rosity, they discover the *great value* of being fused together in Oneness, and, like Abram, they are "*blessed...of God Most High*" (Gen. 14:19).

The economy of Worthless' world operates according to his own **lawless** nature of self-worthship. Jesus warned that "many will **fall away** and will **betray** one another and **hate** one another [*relational fission*].... Because **lawlessness** [*self-indulgence, predatory opportunism*] is increased, most people's **love** [*gene-rosity and fuse-ability*] **will grow cold** [*precipitating darkness, eclipse, and famine*] (Matt. 24:10-12).

Gifts to Captives

God Most High *penetrated* our eclipse and opened the economy of heaven to us: "When **Jesus ascended on high**, He led captive a host of **captives**, and He **gave gifts to men**" (Eph. 4:8; Ps. 68:18). When the Son of Man *ascended* as our Advocate, a lot happened for us, but we will focus on three things—slaves of Christ, transformation of desire, and investment capital.

First, we were formerly *captives* of Worthless' labor-camp, but now we are *captives* of Christ— "**slaves of Christ**" (Eph. 6:6). Since complete individual autonomy [*I am my own master*] is *itself* the lie and a mirage, human beings have only two choices: belonging to the *false-father* who is in the world or belonging to the *true Father* who is in Christ. The **independent renegade** who believes he answers to no one but himself is more a **slave** to Worthless than he realizes; inebriated by self-focus and self-indulgence, he is a self-deceived deceiver and an unwitting pawn of the false-father.

Second, Jesus effects a **transformation of desire**—*desiring desire* itself *for* self (*eros*) is *displaced* by desire to add to God and one another by sacrificial self-giving: "**the *Agape* of Christ controls us**" (2 Cor. 5:14). Your corrupt nature cannot be fixed or cured, it must be *displaced* by a new nature; salvation is essentially "*re-gene-ration*" (Matt. 19:28; Titus 3:5). When your *desire* is transformed, the leash by which the false-father has held you is effectively *severed*. **Worthless' yoke upon your neck is broken**—and Jesus' *Own* testimony becomes *yours*: "the ruler of the world [*Worthless*] …has nothing in Me" (John 14:30).

Third, God's sacrificial Self-giving to us in Christ serves as the **initial investment of capital** required to jump-start the economy of the kingdom [*reciprocal gene-rosity*] among us ransomed captives. In other words, God **gave gifts** to each one of us so we could start giving to one another. Paul observed, "**What do you have** that you did not **receive**? And if you did receive it, why do you boast as if you had not received it?" (1 Cor. 4:7).

[8]And God [*Most High*] is able to make all grace abound to you, so that **always having all sufficiency in everything** [*God's superabundant bounty: investment capital*], you may have **an abundance for every good deed** [*acts of sacrificial self-giving/sharing*]; ...[10]Now He who **supplies** seed to the sower [*giver*] and bread for food will supply and **multiply** your seed for sowing [*exponential fruit-bearing*] and increase the harvest of your righteousness [*maturity in gene-rous DNA*]; [11]you will be **enriched** in everything [*natural and spiritual*] **for all liberality** [*extravagant gene-rosity*], which through us [*heirs/stewards*] is **producing** thanksgiving to God [*jump-starts reciprocal gene-rosity from others to God: expansive growth of the kingdom economy*] (2 Cor. 9:8-11).

Since Father, Son, and Spirit are Self-givers and Self-sharers, we will always *receive* from Them, yet They have purposed to do much more for us than simply giving repeated handouts to us like **welfare-recipients**. The Triune-God desires to plant, cultivate, and mature within each of us the gift of Their own *gene-rous* nature that will enable us, individually and corporately, to ***gene-rate* bounty** in the Trinity-like way of reciprocal gene-rosity. These are *re-gene-rated* dirt bags. Where, precisely, does this supply of seed to the sower [*giver*] come from? The **infusion of capital** necessary to jump-start the economy of the kingdom among us comes from Jesus who is both our inexhaustible Source and economic Advisor:

> [27]Do not work for the **food which perishes** [*full-time in Worthless' labor-camp for self-preservation*], but for the **food which endures to eternal life** [*eating and assimilating Jesus together*], which the Son of Man will **give** [*as capital*] to you.... [51]**I AM the living bread** [*three Ingredients mixed and baked by Agape into One Cake*] **that came down out of heaven...** [*Source of the Trinity's own gene-rous DNA that jump-starts reciprocal gene-rosity and fruit-bearing bounty*] (John 6:27, 51).

Seek First His

When Jesus began His public ministry, He proclaimed *the Sermon on the Mount* as an **inaugural address** of the coming of the kingdom of God into the world. As we survey this brilliant yet practical revelation, it is remarkable to discover that **economics** is the primary theme. Jesus began *penetrating* the eclipse of the fallen world by shining the Light of the knowledge of the Triune-Most High into the hearts and minds of weary and heavy-laden captives of its corrupt economy—Worthless' labor-camp. Here, at the very beginning of His ministry, Jesus unveiled the essential **master-key of kingdom economics: "seek first His."** After His address, this God-Man invested three years serving as our Mentor to demonstrate for us how to do it:

> [24]No one [*individual*] can serve two masters [*fuse into two nuclei at once*]; for either he will **hate** the one [*God in Christ*] and **love** the other [*self-worth-ship*], or he will be **devoted** to one [*perpetually fused into the Nucleus of the Trinity*] and **despise** the other [*"hate" his own self-indulgent life in this world" John 12:25*]. **You cannot serve God** [*kingdom economy*] **and wealth** [*lit. mammon; Worthless' economy*]. [25]For this reason I say to you, **do not be worried** [*self-conscious*] **about your life** [*how will I preserve and provide for self?*], as to what you will eat or what you will drink; nor for your body, as to what you will put on. Is not **life** [*reciprocal self-giving Love*] more than food, and the **body** [*soil for the seed; temple for spiritual fusion*] more than clothing? [26]**Look at the birds of the air**, that they do not sow, nor reap nor gather into barns, and yet your heavenly **Father feeds** them. Are you not **worth** much more than they? [30]...You of **little faith!** [*eclipsed from reality: the gene-rous nature and bountiful economy of God Most High*]

³¹**Do not worry then**, saying, "What will we eat? ...drink? ...wear for clothing?" ³²**For the Gentiles** [*dispirited dirt-bags*] **eagerly seek all these things** [*buying and selling one another as opportunists to procure things below–dirt*]; for your heavenly **Father knows** that you need all these things. But **seek first His** kingdom [*individuals in fusion Oneness*] and **His** righteousness [*sacrificial self-giving*], and all these [*natural*] things will be **added** to you (Matt. 6:24-33).

The secret of the mystery of the kingdom of God is summed up in these three words—"**seek first His**"—because Father, Son, and Spirit always *seek first* the interest of One Another and together, as One God, these Three always *seek first* our interests. "God in Christ" is a **Triune-Groom** who came to lay down His life for us, His **many-membered bride**. Our Triune-Groom sacrificially *expended* Himself for us not because He wanted to *take* something from us but because He wanted to *give* to us. The Triune-God of *Agape* created mankind as an "other" simply so He could *seek first* ours: "so that in the **ages to come** He might show the **surpassing riches** of His grace in kindness toward us [*gene-rously cherishing and adding to His bride*] in Christ Jesus" (Eph. 2:7).

The **prime directive** for every individual who participates in the economy of the kingdom is "**seek**

first His." This can only be properly understood as **pure stewardship**: giving all that I am to *give* Him what *He* wants and to make sure *His* will is accomplished. In other words, **my desire is simply to fulfill His desire**. Inferred in this stewardship is a childlike faith in God's *gene-rous* and thoughtful nature: you know He has already included you in His desire because you are *His* treasure just as He is *yours*, and He has already made the fullest provision for your care. Since it is impossible to out-give God, you are entirely *free* to be "**rich toward God**" (Luke 12:21)—recklessly extravagant in *gene-rosity* to Him, as well as to other human beings whom God desires to enrich *through* you! In *eros* rationale, this economic plan seems like foolishness, yet it actually works! It is obvious that we individualists could never live as Trinity-like stewards apart from *re-gene-ration*—"becoming **partakers of the divine nature** [*gene-rous DNA*], having escaped the **corruption** that is in the world by **lust** [*desiring desire, self-worth-ship*]." (2 Pet. 1:4).

In Jesus' Own understanding (*Agape* rationale), the *primary* reason He came into the world as "the Son of Man [*our Representative*]" (Luke 19:10) was to "*seek first His*" as a Man: "For I have come down from heaven, **not to do My own will, but the will of Him who sent Me**" (John 6:38). We human beings were born seeking first *our own* desire, and as we age, the tyranny of self-will only becomes more sophisticated. For the sake of *willful* mankind, the Man Jesus sweat blood in the garden, and *on our behalf* He said to

Father, "**not My will, but *Yours* be done**" (Luke 22:42). What we could not do, the God-Man "did" (Rom. 8:3). To enter and participate in the kingdom, it is not possible to overemphasize how essential it is to "seek first His." Abraham, the wise emigrant to the kingdom, meditated and acted upon this prime directive each day of his life and found himself *in* and *of* God Most High. T. Austin Sparks described this kingdom way of life:

> Where and how shall we find the Lord? Only on the line of Christ, where **Christ's interests are the object of our being here** [*seek first His*], where it is true "For me to live is Christ" (Phil. 1:21). You find the Lord there. Get off that ground, be driven off, be allured off, and you **lose** the Lord. It is there, on that ground, that the explanation of the Christian life [*in the kingdom*] is found. It is on that line that the very purpose for which we are created will have its out-working. It is on that line that we shall find divine guidance.

> This Divine law of **God's way** [*Three mutually exalting One Another*] has many practical applications in the life of the Christian. How many spiritual tragedies we have known brought about by **human selectiveness apart from the first and**

supreme interest of Christ. It might be the choice of residence, location, for instance, for reasons of convenience, pleasure, escape, or seeming necessity.... No less a question than having the Lord with us is bound up with such **choices and decisions**. We cannot move off the Lord's ground [*buying the lie, chasing mirages, upward descent*] without the **consequence of spiritual disaster** [*fission, con-fusion, eclipse, famine*]....

If Christ is the Way [*downward ascent*], the Directive [*seek first His*]; then He is the Example. How **meticulously careful** He was not to move, or be moved by any consideration but **the directive of the Father!** [*"...that the world may know I Agape the Father, I do exactly as the Father commanded Me" John 14:31*] Many motives were put to Him for action and movement, but He abode in the Father [*altruism*], and, often at great cost [*Self-denial*], refused other considerations [*refused to sell*].[4]

Jesus said, "whoever wishes to **save his life** [*e.g. look out for #1*] **will lose it** [*upward descent*]; but

[4] Sparks, T. Austin. (n.d.). *The Line of Christ*, retrieved from http://www.austin-sparks.net/english/books/002765.html.

whoever **loses his life for My sake** [*seek first His*] **will find it** [*downward ascent into God Most High*]" (Matt. 16:25). To *buy into* the kingdom, you must *sell* your own autonomous life and *seek first His*, but the new life you "find" is in the Nucleus (cohabitation) of Three burden-bearers who selflessly and conscientiously care for One Another and for you! "He who dwells in **the shelter of the Most High** [*Holy, Holy, Holy*] will **abide** in the shadow of the Almighty [*All-Three-Mighty*]" (Ps. 91:1). To *remain* in the Nucleus, which Jesus called "abiding," you cannot take the extravagant blessings God gives you, and own them or spend them on yourself; rather, you must *continue* to *seek first His* as a steward and spend *all* you receive *from* Him *on* Him. Peter described the economy of the kingdom this way:

> [5]...all of you clothe yourselves with **humility** toward one another [*practice Trinity-likeness; "be imitators of God" Eph. 5:1*], for God is opposed to the **proud** [*self-centered*] but gives grace to the **humble** [*steward-hearted*]. [6]Therefore humble yourselves under the mighty hand of God, that He may **exalt** you at the proper time, [7]**casting all your anxiety on Him** [*utterly forgetting your own cares*], because He cares for you (1 Pet. 5:5-7).

In the kingdom of Triune-*Agape*, the *eros* instinct of self-preservation is not only unnecessary, it is counter-productive; there is no need to **look out for #1** because others do it for you, even as you look out for them. *Agape* "does not seek its own" (1 Cor. 13:5). Paul added, "**Do nothing from selfishness or empty conceit** [*self-worth-ship*], but with **humility** of mind [*Agape rationale*] **regard one another as more important than yourselves** [*Trinity-likeness*]; do not merely look out for **your own personal interests**, but also for **the interests of others**" (Phil. 2:3-4).

In the God-Man Nucleus, you do not need to waste one minute worrying about your own needs because God has *already* anticipated them freeing you to *invest* all your time into *seeking first His* interests as a steward-son. In Worthless' marketplace, we act as *eros opportunists* for **self-indulgence**; in the kingdom, we are *Agape opportunists*—always seeking an occasion to *add to* one another by our own **self-expenditure** (see Phil. 4:10). This abundant life of reciprocal burden-bearing and care—*seeking first one another's*—is what the Scriptures call **entering into God's rest** (see Heb. 4:1). T. Austin Sparks described the implications:

> Christ is God's Sabbath [*Nucleus of the Trinity's rest*]. Christ is our Sabbath [*Nucleus of the Trinity's rest opened to us*]. When we enter by faith into Christ's righteousness [*reciprocal Self-giving and burden-bearing*], **we enter into God's rest** [*relational Oneness, perichoresis*]. It is a tremendous **power** [*fusion*]....

The Lord says, in quite simple language, "If only you will **trust Me** [*buy into the Triune-Most High*], and trust My provision [*gene-rous bounty*], and stop worrying, stop fretting, stop being anxious [*self-conscious*]; if you will but **believe Me** [*Three all-true to One Another and to you*], I have the ground upon which I could **meet all your need** [*kingdom bounty*]...if only you will **rest in Me** to bring you through [*into God Most High*], you will be saved from so much of this weakness, and fret, and anxiety!" **Worry** [*self-consciousness*] **is a destroying thing** [*fission decay*]. At the back of a lot that we suffer in body, and in mind, there is so often a secret, hidden **restlessness** [*desiring desire*], something deep down in our subconscious being of a [*self-focused*] fret, an anxiety, something that is **not rest** [*freedom from the tyranny of self*]. It takes many forms.... But to recognise Christ as God's rest [*Nucleus*] through righteousness [*reciprocal sacrificial self-giving*], to observe that, to keep that Sabbath, is **life** [*Agape–fusion*] **which conquers death** [*eros–fission*]....[5]

[5] Sparks, T. Austin (n.d.) *Spiritual Ministry*, Chapter 4 – The Ministration of Condemnation and the Ministration of Righteousness. Retrieved from http://www.austin-sparks.net/english/books/003257.html.

The rest, which individuals enjoy in the kingdom, is *not* the passivity and idleness of **careless** welfare recipients; rather, in freedom from self-interest, each individual is *free* to **care** for one another—the **active rest** of participating in the economy of the kingdom as fellow burden-bearers. Active rest *facilitates* a cohabitation of peace that is the ideal greenhouse environment for the growth of **in-gen-uity**—God's own creativity manifested in us and through us—and true **fruit-bearing** (see John 15:1-16).

Solomon observed, "One hand full of **rest** is better [*more productive*] than two fists full of **labor and striving after wind** [*Worthless' mirage; futility*]" (Eccl. 4:6). Entering God's rest means you are *free* from the anxiety of self-interest, self-sourcing, and self-preservation; therefore, you are *free* to share as a co-laborer with God in His own creative and invigorating work of fruit-bearing *gene-rosity*. Paul wrote to Timothy, "…we **labor and strive** because we have fixed our hope on the **living God** [*Three alive to One Another*]" (1 Tim. 4:10). As immature, untrained stewards, we must learn to *labor* together "according to the [*fusion*] power that works within us" (Eph. 3:20).

It is not possible to *seek first His* unless we truly **understand what God wants**. As we come to *know* Father, Son, and Spirit, we discover the *foremost* desire of our Triune-God is that you and I and Their other kids learn to *seek first one another's* in a Trinity-like way and thereby **manifest the fusion glory of the kingdom together**. Paul advised, "Owe nothing to anyone except to *Agape* one another; for he who loves [*sacrificially gives himself to*] his neighbor has fulfilled the law [*Trinity-likeness*]" (Rom. 13:8). To seek first His kingdom and His righteousness means **seeking first *His interests* in one another** in such a way that yields superabundant bounty both of relational "fullness" and the material resources to give and share with others. Paul described how believers in Macedonia were *maturing* in Trinity-likeness by *practicing* kingdom economics:

> [1]Now, brethren, we wish to make known to you the grace of God which has been given in the churches of Macedonia, [2]that **in a great ordeal of affliction** [*circumstances of famine*] **their abundance of joy and** their **deep poverty overflowed in the wealth of their liberality** [*superabundant gene-rosity*]. [3]For I testify that according to their ability, and **beyond their ability**, they gave of their own accord [*from a willing spirit*], [4]begging us with much urging for the favor of **participation in the support of the saints**, [5]and this, not as we had expected, but they **first gave themselves to the Lord and to us** [*fused together into the Nucleus of the God-Man Jesus*] by the will of God [*seeking first His*] (2 Cor. 8:1-5).

Though this famine brought hardship, it also provided a marvelous opportunity for the translocal body of Christ in the first century to *discover* the bountiful economy of the kingdom, to *mature* in reciprocal gene-rosity, and to *grow* exponentially in the quality and quantity of their relationships. Paul also stated this:

> [26]Macedonia and Achaia have been pleased to make a **contribution** for the poor among the saints in Jerusalem [*in famine*]. [27]Yes, they were **pleased** to do so [*not from duty, obligation or coercion, but manifesting God's true, gene-rous nature*], and they are indebted to them. For if the Gentiles have **shared** in their spiritual things, they are **indebted** [*by the law of the kingdom: reciprocal gene-rosity*] to **minister** to them also in material things (Rom. 15:26-27).

In Worthless' marketplace, we are *con-fused* to other opportunists for the purpose of more effectively exploiting and taking from the unsuspecting so we can get our share of the profits. In the kingdom, we are *fused* together into Christ for an **extroverted purpose**—to join our Triune-God in extravagant *gene-rosity* not only to one another but also to those who are still **captives of Worthless' labor-camp**. We who have *bought into* Christ must *first* learn reciprocal gene-rosity with one another, and then we must gather up the bounty it produces and **invest** it into those weary and heavy laden captives still languishing in Worthless' yoke! Paul urged Timothy, "…join with me [*fusion*] in suffering for the gospel [*sacrificially carrying God's invitation to lose your life and fuse into Christ*] according to the [*fusion*] power of God" (2 Tim. 1:8). Jesus dispatched His disciples into the world to *practice* the principles of kingdom economics that He had taught them:

> ⁷As you **go**, preach, saying, "**The kingdom of heaven** [*economy of God Most High*] is at hand." ⁸**...Freely you have received** [*Agape*], **freely give** [*reciprocate God's gene-rosity by sacrificial self-giving to all mankind*]. ⁹**Do not acquire** gold, or silver, or copper for your money belts [*eros economy*], ¹⁰or a bag for your journey... for the worker [*steward-son*] is worthy of his support [*lit. nourishment*] (Matt. 10:5-10).

Jesus assigned this life-lab to His disciples so they could *test* this counter-intuitive economic plan in real-life situations while He was absent from them. The Master purposed for them to *seek first His* interests in others with **radical abandon** and discover that God had already anticipated all their needs in the *exact* same way God anticipated Him in all the signs and miracles of *gene-rosity* He performed while they were watching. He desired for them to **practice** kingdom economics so they would **grow** from faith to faith, and from life to life and from glory to glory into **mature** sons of the Most High:

³²If you love those who love you, what **credit** is that to you [*in the economy of the kingdom*]? For even sinners [*individualists*] love those who love them [*reciprocal eros payoff; con-fusion*].... ³⁴If you **lend** to those from whom you **expect to receive**, what **credit** is that to you? For even sinners do the same. Even sinners lend to sinners in order to **receive back** the same amount. ³⁵But **Agape** [*sacrificially give yourself to*] **your enemies** [*predatory opportunists*], and do good [*unconditional gene-rosity*], and **lend, expecting nothing in return** [*do not seek eros payoffs*]; and your **reward** will be great [*Life in mutual exaltation; a reciprocal inheritance*], and **you will be sons of the Most High**; for He Himself is kind to ungrateful and evil men (Luke 6:32-35; see also Luke 14:14).

Sons of the Most High

The Incarnate Son Jesus was born innocent and sinless, yet He had to be tested and proven incorruptible and righteous (mature in *Agape*) as a Man in order to be "made perfect" (Heb. 7:28) and to **"be called** [*recognized as*] **the Son of the Most High God"** (Luke 1:32; Mark 5:7). When Jesus had passed His final exam at the cross—offering His body, soul, and spirit in comprehensive, sacrificial Self-giving—

"He was **declared the Son of God** [*Most High*] with power by the resurrection from the dead, according to the Spirit of holiness, Jesus Christ our Lord" (Rom. 1:4). Not only did the **Spirit** certify that the Man Jesus was *perfected* in God's Own holy, incorruptible, fuse-able DNA, but the **Roman executioner** also certified this: "When the centurion, who was standing right in front of Him [*at the cross*], saw the way He breathed His last, he said, '**Truly this man was the Son of God!**'" (Mark 15:39).

> [8]Although He was a Son, He **learned obedience** [*to "seek first His" by self-denial and sacrificial self-giving*] from the things which He suffered. [9]And having been **made perfect**, He became to all those who obey Him **the source** of eternal salvation [*re-gene-rative Seed*] (Heb. 5:8-9).

The Son was *already* perfect in eternity, "existing in the form of God" (Phil. 2:6), yet He became **our Forerunner Man** to make a journey of downward ascent ahead of us to *become* "a Son, made perfect forever" (Heb. 7:28). Father purposed for the Man Jesus to become **the prototype Son of the Most High** that we might be "**conformed** [*lit. Greek: summorphos; morphed*] to the image of His Son, so that He would be the firstborn among many brethren [*sons and daughters of the Most High*]" (Rom. 8:29; also see Phil. 3:10).

No human being has ever emerged from his or her mother's womb as a son or daughter of the Most High; each are **purchased slaves** whom God in Christ freed from Worthless' yoke, progressively sanctified, *re-gene-rated*, and disciplined into the *gene-rous*, fuse-able nature of the Triune-God. Each one is **mentored** in sacrificial self-giving, **tested** in self-denial through acute suffering, **trained** in reciprocal gene-rosity, and **matured** from faith to faith and from glory to glory into the image of Jesus.

Paul wrote, "Just as we have borne the image of the **earthy** [*de-gene-rate dirt-bags*], we will also bear the image of the **heavenly** [*re-gene-ration in the likeness of the Triune-Most High*]" (1 Cor. 15:49). Each of these redeemed captives whom God transformed into "sons [*and daughters*] of the Most High" (Luke 6:35) were formerly dispirited dirt-bags who practiced self-worship in Worthless world, but then Jesus, Son of the Most High God, intervened. They recognized Him as *gen-uine* treasure, *bought into* Him and received "**the upward call of God in Christ Jesus**" (Phil. 3:14). They willingly followed Jesus *out* of Worthless' world and *into* God Most High, making many mistakes along the way! "Therefore, **holy brethren** [*born into Jesus' bloodline: incorruptible, fuse-able DNA*], **partakers of a heavenly calling** [*participation in the economy and life of the Most High*], **consider Jesus** [*our Forerunner Man and Master: exalted as the God-Man Nucleus*]…" (Heb. 3:1).

Considering Jesus involves more than simply seeing Him as an example; in a practical sense it means to be *considerate* of Him—to "seek first His" as a steward who conscientiously attends to His interests as a **bond-servant** of Jesus Christ (see Rom. 1:1; 2 Pet. 1:1). Until we are "clothed with power from on high [*filled with the Spirit–the Re-gene-rator*]" (Luke 24:49), we cannot *seek first His* and mature as stewards; "**For all who are being led by the Spirit of God** [*Most High*], **these are sons of God** [*Most High*]" (Rom. 8:14). As we receive and practice yielding ourselves to "the Spirit of Christ" (Rom. 8:9), we grow and mature as "**sons of the living God** [*Three alive to One Another*]" (Rom. 9:26).

The Spirit constantly seeks out His wayward sons and daughters; again and again He finds us lying in the dirt, covered in Worthless' ashes, and drunk on "old wine [*self-indulgence*]" (Luke 5:39). He sobers us up from our intoxicated condition, He systematically *de-fuses* our *con-fusion* to the false-father and other opportunists, and He awakens us to our true origin and home: "A glorious throne on **high** from the beginning [*eternal Triune-kingdom*] is the place of our sanctuary [*rest*]" (Jer. 17:12). By progressively **transforming our insatiable desire into desire for God**, the Spirit helps us *relocate* our treasure, affections, and consciousness *into* God Most High. As soon as wayward sons begin to *yield* to the Spirit, "they **desire a better country, that is**, **a heavenly one**. Therefore God is not ashamed to be called their God; for He has prepared a city [*cohabitation*] for them" (Heb. 11:16).

The Spirit of God Most High **acculturates** us into His kingdom by *mentoring* us in kingdom economics; it is the Spirit *within* us Who spontaneously moves us to say, "Worthy are You, our Lord and our God, to receive glory and honor and power [*our reciprocal gene-rosity*]" (Rev. 4:11). The Spirit is constantly and actively **conforming** (morphing) our nature and behavior into the likeness of Jesus, Son of the Most High God, and we *become* "**heirs of God and fellow-heirs with Christ**" (Rom. 8:17). Paul added, "The creation [*enslaved in corruption*] waits eagerly for **the revealing of the** [*incorruptible*] **sons** of God" (Rom. 8:19). Daniel prophesied, "**The saints of the Highest One** [*children acculturated into the economy of God Most High*] will **receive the kingdom** [*fusion cohabitation*] and **possess the kingdom** [*as steward-heirs*] forever, for all ages to come" (Dan. 7:18).

The **custody battle,** which the false-father wages for God's adopted sons and daughters, is very severe because there is so much at stake—we are heirs of a vast estate. This is a cautionary lesson learned from the fall of both Adam and Esau. As a shrewd thief, opportunist, and usurper, Worthless targets immature, *wayward* sons because we are such easy prey. An heir who is intoxicated by insatiable desire will *recklessly* jump at any opportunity for self-indulgence and *carelessly* **sell his inheritance for a single meal** (see Heb. 12:16).

T. Austin Sparks explained the implications of this custody battle:

> The one great effort of the enemy, which is again and again successful...has been to **bring the things of God down** to the attachment with this world [*confusion*], attachment to the earth [*terra firma*], **to make them something here** [*of value in Worthless' eros economy*]. ... you need only to read John to see how unattached everything [*of the kingdom*] is, how everything is **lifted clean out of this world** [*out of the dirt*], and everything is bound up with the fact that Christ [*the God-Man Nucleus*] is in heaven, and that the Lord's people are here, but not here, here, but not known, in the world, but not of it; **a mystery people in this world** so far as the world is concerned [*living daily in a transcendent Reality eclipsed to the world*]...yet by that very means and for that very reason, the **most potent force** that this universe knows: the spiritual, hidden, secret people of God in this earth [*sons and daughters of God Most High*].

To take hold of Christianity and mould it, and shape it, and systematise it, and crystallise it, and make it some mighty

Movement here; with its **roots here** [*in the dirt*], with all its associations such as man can see, appreciate, and approve; to register itself upon the **ordinary consciousness of this world** as being something [*of value in Worthless' marketplace*]; all of that is contrary to the Word of God and is **contrary to spiritual life** [*kingdom economics: reciprocal, self-expenditure*] **and spiritual power** [*self-emptied individuals in fusion*]. Christ is in heaven [*Nucleus of the Most High*], and **we are lifted out**....[6]

The Bible is essentially a collection of stories of individuals from various generations whom the Spirit of the Triune-God *led* into the relational, fusion dynamic of reciprocal-generosity and mutual exaltation. By the way of *downward ascent*, these dirt-bags were **transformed** into sons and daughters and **lifted** by the Spirit into God Most High. Old Testament saints such as "Enoch, in the seventh generation from Adam" (Jude 14) and Noah and Isaiah *saw forward* to Christ "through the eternal Spirit" (Heb. 9:14) and *bought into* Him by faith. A number of **women** practiced *reciprocal gene-rosity* with God and became *daughters of the Most High* such as Ruth, Hannah, Abigail, Mary Magdalene, Mary the mother of Jesus, Lydia, etc. As a very young **child**, "Samuel was lying

6 Spark, T. Austin (n.d.). *That Which Was From The Beginning.* "Chapter 1 – God's Beginning Governs His End" retrieved from http://www.austin-sparks.net/english/books/002953.html

down in the temple of the Lord where the ark was" (1 Sam. 3:3); God called to Samuel, raised him as His Own *incorruptible* son and lifted him into the Most High (see 1 Sam. 12:3).

For the purpose of illustrating **how God mentors men in kingdom economics**, we will look briefly at Abraham, Joseph, David, Daniel, Nebuchadnezzar, and Paul.

Abram of God Most High

Centuries before the Son was incarnated into human flesh as the Man Jesus, He came down to the earth to meet Abram as a *theophany* (God appearing in human form; see Heb. 7). The eternal Son came to bless Abram with an **investment of capital** that would jump-start Abram's participation in the economy of the kingdom of God Most High:

> [18]Melchizedek king of Salem [*lit. king of peace; pre-incarnate Son*] brought out **bread** and **wine** [*sacrificial Self-giving: investment capital*]; now He was **priest** [*Steward-Son*] **of God Most High**. [19]He blessed him and said, "**Blessed be Abram of God Most High**, possessor of heaven and earth...." [*Abram lit. exalted father*] [20]**gave Him a tenth of all** [*reciprocal gene-rosity*]. [21]The king of Sodom [*son of Worthless*] said to Abram, "**Give the people to me** and **take the goods for**

yourself [*eros economics*]." ²²Abram said to the king of Sodom, "I have sworn [*lit. given my life in pledge*] to the **Lord God Most High**, possessor of heaven and earth [*a fusion agreement*], ²³that **I will not take** a thread or a sandal thong or anything that is yours, for fear you would say, 'I have made Abram rich' [*diminishing God's worth and glory*]'" (Gen. 14:18-23).

Abram *bought into* "God is true" and refused to *sell*; therefore, he himself could not be bought. Because Abram willingly forfeited his life in fusion into the Nucleus of the Son, he was unleashed from Worthless' lie, nature, and world economy. Abram learned to seek first His and was tested and proven **incorruptible**. He became a **steward** into whose care God could entrust His most precious possession—the seed of the son of promise, which was Jesus Himself, born through the lineage of Isaac. As Abraham *practiced* sacrificial self-giving and *matured* in reciprocal gene-rosity, he was ready for his **final exam in kingdom economics**— participating in God's ultimate plan of salvation by *willingly* and *sacrificially* **offering up Isaac**, his only son whom he loved (see Gen. 22:2).

To commemorate Abram's maturity as a steward-son *of the Most High*, God changed his name to "Abraham [*lit. father of a multitude of nations*]" (Gen. 17:4-5). Further, "Abraham...was called the **friend** of God" (James 2:23). Both God and Abraham greatly *cherished* the relationship of reciprocal gene-rosity that they shared in fusion, and it continued **bearing fruit even to his offspring**. Even after Abraham was dead, God never stopped *seeking first* to add to him and exalt him by sacrificially *giving* to and *forgiving* his corrupt, wayward descendants, saying, "**for the sake of My servant Abraham**" (Gen. 26:24). "In Christ Jesus [*the promised seed*] **the blessing of Abraham** [*reciprocal gene-rosity with God Most High*] might **come to the Gentiles**, so that we would receive the promise of the Spirit [*re-gene-ration in fuse-able DNA*] through faith" (Gal. 3:14).

Abraham's great-grandson, **Joseph**, became a unique sharer in this inheritance because God also exalted him as a son of the Most High. At age seventeen, he kept receiving dreams from the Lord that his father, mother, and brothers would bow down to him (see Gen. 37). Yet, this naïve young man could not possibly have imagined the thirteen-year interim of suffering, betrayal, and **emptying** in downward ascent that lay ahead to transform him into a steward and conduit through whom the *gene-rous* **bounty** of the Most High could be poured out in the midst of **worldwide famine**.

> [9]The patriarchs [*Joseph's brothers*] became **jealous of** Joseph and **sold** him into Egypt. Yet God [*Most High*] was with Him, [10]and rescued him from all his afflictions, and granted him favor and wisdom [*Agape*

rationale] in the sight of Pharaoh, king of Egypt, and he made him **governor** over Egypt and all his household (Acts 7:9-10).

In preparation to become a steward-son of the Most High, Joseph was disowned, falsely accused, imprisoned, forgotten, broken, and thoroughly *emptied* in order that he might be *filled* with *Agape*: "They afflicted his feet with fetters, **he himself** [*self-will*] **was laid in irons**; until the time that his word [*prophetic dreams*] came to pass, the word of the Lord **tested** him" (Ps. 105:18-19). God progressively mentored Joseph in kingdom economics by investing him into four different **houses of stewardship training**: Jacob's house, Potiphar's house, the jail house, and Pharaoh's house. Joseph was broken upon "the cornerstone" (Matt. 21:42-44) and learned to *seek first His*; therefore, God Most High **exalted** him from prisoner to prime minister in just a few hours. As the seven-year famine became more severe, the only food on the entire continent was that which Joseph had stored up in Egypt; therefore, **Joseph governed the entire world economy as a bond-servant of God Most High**.

Joseph's entire family relocated to Egypt into his provision and care; shortly thereafter his father, Jacob, died. Once Joseph and his brothers buried their father, these opportunists who had been **jealous of** him became afraid saying, "What if Joseph bears a grudge against us and **pays us back in full** for all the wrong which we did to him!" (Gen. 50:15). Joseph had suffered all *twelve stages of relational fission* at the hands of these treacherous brothers who disowned him and sold him into slavery. Now, prostrate before Joseph, they had come to the bitter end of their *upward descent*. As the ruler of Egypt, Joseph had both the authority and opportunity to execute them, imprison them, or simply to deny them grain and let them to starve to death. However, the Triune-God had comprehensively **emptied Joseph of self-worth-ship and opportunism** and *filled* him with Their own true, **jealous-for** nature, which "is kind to ungrateful and **evil men**" (Luke 6:35). As a son of God Most High mentored in kingdom economics, *giving* and *forgiving* was Joseph's spontaneous, *gen-uine* response:

> [19]"Do not be afraid, for **am I in God's place?** [*e.g. am I an unbroken nucleus of self-will, self-worth-ship – making myself like the Most High?*] [20]As for you, you meant **evil** [*eros*] against me, but God meant it for **good** [*Agape*] in order to bring about this present result, to preserve many people alive [*type of Christ*]. [21]...I will **provide** [*gene-rously*] for you and your little ones." So he comforted them and spoke kindly to them (Gen. 50:19-21).

In true worth-ship, Joseph reflected upon all his suffering and losses with contentment because **God's purposes and interests** were all that mattered to him.

Further, Joseph was never dazzled by his high position or the vast resources [*mammon*] at his disposal. Nor was he interested in being *con-fused* to Egypt as an emigrant citizen or loyal advocate of the land where his very *name* carried the incalculable **equity of high esteem**. Joseph's heart, mind, soul, and strength were wholly fused into God Most High and his allegiance, true treasure, and emigrant destination *remained* **the inheritance of the stewardship of God's promise**:

> [24]Joseph said to his brothers, "I am about to die, but God [*Three burden-bearers*] will surely **take care of you** and bring you up from this land [*Egypt*] to the land which He promised on oath to Abraham, to Isaac and to Jacob. [25]Then Joseph made the sons of Israel swear, saying, '…**you shall carry my bones up from here**" (Gen. 50:24-25).

David: The Man Who Was Raised On High

Over his lifetime, David was many things: youngest of nine brothers who demeaned him; **shepherd boy** and **psalmist** whom God anointed through Samuel to be the future king; victor over Goliath; captain of the Israeli army; King Saul's son-in-law and the object of his murderous envy; desperate fugitive; defector to Israel's enemy, the Philistines; crowned king of Judah and Israel; visionary of Zion [*an earthly micro-model of the heavenly kingdom of priests*]; architect of God's temple; adulterer, murderer, and man of earnest repentance; and zealous **worth-shipper** of God.

From these life-labs and experiences, David certainly knew something about *desiring desire*, upward descent, and the twelve stages of **relational fission** both as a victim and as an offender. However, David also practiced reciprocal gene-rosity with God Most High and became a **fusion pioneer** way ahead of his time. Through the eternal Spirit, David saw forward to Christ, *bought into* Him, and enjoyed a New Testament quality of spiritual life even while he was still technically under the Law of Moses. At the end of his remarkable and turbulent life, he wrote:

> [1]Now these are the last words of David… **the man who was raised on high** [*into relationship with God Most High by downward ascent*]…the sweet psalmist of Israel, [2]"the Spirit of the Lord spoke by me, and His word was on my tongue. …[3]The **Rock** of Israel [*Three fused in incorruptible, unshakable Agape*] spoke to me [*e.g. mentored me in kingdom economics*], 'He who rules over men righteously [*as a sacrificial self-giver*], who rules in the fear of God [*as an incorruptible steward*] [4]is as the **light** of the morning when the **sun** rises [*God is Light and God is a sun–Three in life-giving fusion*], a morning without clouds [*Agape without*

hypocrisy], when the tender grass springs out of the earth through **sunshine after the rain** [*photosynthesis*]. ⁵Truly is not **my house so with God?** [*cohabitation of God and man mutually indwelling one another*] For He has made an everlasting **covenant** [*fusion agreement*] with me, ordered in all things, and **secured** [*on the Rock: in the Son, through the cross, by the Spirit*]; for all my salvation [*re-gene-ration*] and all my **desire** [*fusion into "God is a dwelling place"*], will He not make it **grow** [*from faith to faith, life to life, glory to glory*]? ⁶But the **worthless** [*de-gene-rate captives of "the father of the lie"*] every one of them will be thrust away like **thorns** [*predatory opportunists mature in Worthless' economy*], because they cannot be taken in hand [*brought near in reciprocal self-giving*], ⁷but the man who touches them must be **armed** with iron and the shaft of a spear [*perpetually on guard, no relational rest or peace*], and they will be completely burned with **fire** in their place [*God is a consuming fire*]'" (2 Sam. 23:1-7).

The Spirit of the Son of God repeatedly visited this shepherd boy in the fields and *awakened* his spirit. Curiously, God *mentored* David in kingdom economics as a psalmist—opening the economy of the

Most High to him through the song of the Lord: "**He put a new song in my mouth** [*investment capital*], **a song of praise** [*reciprocal gene-rosity*] **to our God**" (Ps. 40:3). The Son of God Most High progressively *filled* David with His very Own Life as a **Steward-Son**—His own affections, economy of worth, words, feelings, and purposes (see Ps. 18, 22). A profound and intimate fusion relationship occurred as David *bought into* the Nucleus of Christ: "I, Jesus…. **I am the root and the descendant of David**, the bright morning star [*Nucleus of the fusion of God and man*]" (Rev. 22:16). David described what this process of relational fusion was like:

> "You have enclosed me behind and before [*in Your Nucleus*], and laid Your hand [*Son*] upon me. Such **knowledge** [*the secret of the mystery*] is too wonderful for me; it is **too high** [*transcendent Reality of God Most High*], **I cannot attain to it** [*e.g. I am still an individualist–an earth-bound dirt-bag not yet fuse-able*]" (Ps. 139:5-6).

David felt grossly inadequate to participate in the kingdom cohabitation God was revealing to him. However, "the Spirit of the Lord came mightily upon David" (1 Sam. 16:13), and through suffering and much trial and error, He trained, tested, and disciplined him as His Own son to *seek first His*. Paul summarized David's life:

²²After He had **removed** him [*Saul who exalted himself*], He **raised up** David to be their king, concerning whom He also testified and said, "I have found David the son of Jesse, **a man after My heart** [*an affectionate, sacrificial self-giving shepherd in the likeness of the Son*], who will **do all My will** [*seek first His*]." ²³From the descendants of this man, according to promise, God has brought to Israel a **Savior**, **Jesus** [*to lift us fallen dirt-bags into the Most High*] (Acts 13:22-23).

The Triune-Most High progressively lifted and exalted David into Themselves by **acculturating** him into the economy of Their kingdom. David wrote, "I will cry to **God Most High**, to God who **accomplishes all things *for* me**" (Ps. 57:2). David discovered that Father, Son, and Spirit are three burden-bearers who add to One Another and *exalt* One Another in *jealous-for* Love. Further, he recognized the superabundant fullness of Triune-Love was reaching down in *jealousy-for* him to transform his *eros* nature and desires, to lift him [*a dirt-bag*] out of all his troubles, and to fuse him into the Most High. David said, "For the king trusts in the Lord [*e.g. invests himself into Three who invest Themselves into One Another*], and through **the lovingkindness of the Most High** [*Triune-solidarity in Agape–the Rock*] he will not be shaken" (Ps. 21:7). David also stated, "Your right hand [*Son*] upholds me [*in the Nucleus of the Triune God*]; and **Your gentleness** [*lit. humility, meekness*] **makes me great** [*e.g. exalts me*]" (Ps. 18:35). This was the secret, fusion-power source of all David's victories and accomplishments.

Father, Son, and Spirit invited David to *participate* in Their true, *jealous-for* Love:

> "Zeal for Your house will consume me [*my autonomous life/nucleus*]" (Ps. 69:9; John 2:17). As a steward-son, David cherished this inheritance and practiced kingdom economics: "**Offer to God** a sacrifice of thanksgiving and **pay your vows** to the Most High; [*God answered:*] **call upon Me** in the day of trouble; **I shall rescue you**, and **you will honor Me** [*reciprocal gene-rosity*] (Ps. 50:14-15). David became *consumed* with honoring God and *seeking first His* saying to Nathan the prophet, "See now, I dwell in a house of cedar, but the ark of God [*Triune-Shekinah*] dwells within tent **curtains**!" (2 Sam. 7:2).

Like his forefathers Abraham and Joseph, David *matured* in his understanding of kingdom economics through embracing difficult life-labs of downward ascent; therefore, he became a *conduit* of the bountiful *gene-rosity* of the Most High into the earth. The Triune-God transformed David from a taker into a sacrificial self-giver: **a steward-son** into whose care They could entrust the priceless seed—*Jesus, Son of* *the Most High God*—through whom Their redemptive purpose would ultimately be fulfilled:

> ²⁰I have found David **My servant**; with **My holy oil** [*Spirit*] I have anointed him, ²¹with whom **My hand** [*Son*] will be established; **My arm** also will strengthen him [*"arm of the Lord" John 12:38 = Son of God manifested in and through David's life*]. ²²The enemy [*Worthless*] will not deceive him, nor the son of wickedness afflict [*allure and ensnare*] him. ²³But I [*Triune-Jealous*] shall crush his adversaries before him, and strike those who hate him. ²⁴**My faithfulness** and **My lovingkindness** [*true Triune-Agape*] will be with him, and **in My name** his horn will be **exalted** [*true triumph is not self-exaltation*]. ²⁶... He will cry to Me, "You are my Father, my God, and the **rock** of my salvation [*Triune-solidarity*]." ²⁷I also shall make him **My firstborn** [*Son Jesus: "firstborn of the dead...of the new creation" Col. 1:15-18*], **the highest of the kings of the earth** [*see Rev. 1:5*]. ²⁸**My lovingkindness** I will keep for him forever, and **My covenant** [*fusion agreement*] shall be confirmed to him. ²⁹So I will establish **his seed** forever and **his throne** as the days of **heaven** [*the pre-incarnate Son established David's*

throne and then sat on it as an incarnated Man!]....³⁶his throne as the **sun** [*Nucleus of perpetual fusion*] before Me... ³⁷and the **witness in the sky** [*natural sun*] **is faithful** [*daily sign of spiritual reality: God is a sun*] (Ps. 89:20-37).

The more David became *acculturated* into the kingdom, life, economy, and purpose of the Triune-Most High, the more he recognized and *hated* the ways and counterfeits of Worthless' world. He grieved for his kinsmen who continually exchanged, sold, and forfeited the unfathomable inheritance that God Most High desired to *share* with them as **sons** to instead invest themselves as **individualists** and predatory opportunists into Worthless' economy:

⁵They do not know [*"God is true"*], nor do they understand [*the Triune-Most High*]; they walk about in **darkness** [*eclipsed by individualism*]; all the foundations of the earth are shaken [*fission*]. ⁶I said, "**You are gods**, and all of you are **sons of the Most High**. ⁷Nevertheless you will die like [*corrupt, de-gene-rate*] men and **fall** like any one of the princes [*forfeiting their inheritance above for self-indulgence in the dirt: upward descent*]" (Ps. 82:5-7).

David did not say *"you are gods"* because he believed we human beings are destined to become deities or that he himself was in any way divine or equal to God; David said this because God—three sacrificial Self-sharers—had so impressed upon him Their *jealous-for* desire to *share* all the fullness of Themselves with mankind as sons and daughters that he could not phrase what it means for us to become "**heirs of God and fellow heirs with Christ**" (Rom. 8:17) in any other way. David was describing to men who had *de-gene-rated* into the instinctual behavior of "four-footed **animals** and crawling creatures" (Rom. 1:23) what their true destiny was as sons *re-gene-rated* into the image of the eternal Son. Curiously, when the Son Jesus came, He repeated David's words. Jesus said,

> ³⁰**I and the Father are one**. ³¹The Jews picked up stones again to stone Him. ³²Jesus answered them, "I showed you many good [*gene-rous*] works from the Father; for which of them are you stoning Me?" ³³The Jews answered Him, "For a good work we do not stone You, but for blasphemy; and because You, being a man, make Yourself out to be God." ³⁴Jesus answered them, "Has it not been written in your Law, 'I said **you are gods**'? ³⁵If he called them gods, to whom the word of God [*Son of the Most High: the seed*] came (and the Scripture cannot be broken), ³⁶ do you say of Him, whom the

Father sanctified and sent into the world, 'You are blaspheming,' because I said, 'I am the Son of God'?" (John 10:30-36).

Daniel: Man of High Esteem

"Nebuchadnezzar, king of **Babylon** [*lit. con-fusion*], came to Jerusalem and besieged it" (Dan. 1:1). The monument of Babylon was **the Tower of Babel** [*lit. con-fusion*] built by Worthless for his own self-exaltation. The false-father established this world empire through unwitting captives such as Nebuchadnezzar who were compelled by his same arrogant, predatory nature. Into this **epicenter** of Worthless' world economy—one, enormous, treacherous lions' den of opportunists—the young man **Daniel** was taken into exile along with his entire tribe of Judah. Daniel had not participated in the sins *[self-worth-ship]* of his people, which moved God to drive them into exile and allow His temple to be ransacked, burned, and destroyed, yet Daniel **embraced the humiliation** of enslavement and servitude with them.

Here, in the midst of Worthless' kingdom of **con-fusion**, God greatly favored Daniel, *mentored* him in kingdom economics, *acculturated* him in the way of downward ascent, *matured* him as **fuse-able son of the Most High**, and greatly *exalted* him in the sight of four consecutive world-emperors. Daniel openly acknowledged that the divine wisdom, administrative ability, and *in-gen-uity* for which he was known, promoted, and invested with great authority by his Gentile captors came directly from **abiding** in the Most High: Daniel "entered his house [*in Babylon*] (now in his roof chamber he had **windows open toward Jerusalem)** [*perpetual magnetism to fuse into God is a dwelling place*]; and he continued **kneeling on his knees three times a day**, praying and giving thanks before his God [*practicing reciprocal gene-rosity with Father, Son, and Spirit*], as he had been doing previously" (Dan. 6:10).

The archangels Gabriel and Michael who were sent to Daniel recognized his *gen-uine* **humility** and comprehensive self-giving to the Triune-God; therefore, they addressed him as "**man of high esteem** [*lit. desirability, preciousness*]" (Dan. 10:11, 19). Daniel's faithful and extravagant worth-ship of the Triune-God caused the kingdom of heaven to become embodied *within* him. *Out from* this steward-son of God Most High, **the Light of the economy of the kingdom flooded Worthless' marketplace**, piercing into all the opportunists who were participating in its *con-fusion*, particularly Nebuchadnezzar.

King Nebuchadnezzar is one of the most fascinating people in the Bible; he is the only Gentile to author a portion of the Scriptures (see Dan. 4:34-37). This arrogant, self-absorbed, individualist and **hot-tempered predator** conquered and ruled the entire known world, yet the Lord loved him, chose him, spoke to him through dreams, and even called him "My servant" (Jer. 43:10). Even Daniel loved Nebuchadnezzar, and the king grew to highly esteem Daniel: "King Nebuchadnezzar **fell on his face and did homage to Daniel**, and gave orders to present to him an **offering and fragrant incense**" (Dan. 2:46). This shrewd, world-class ruler perceived the rare fragrance of the broken, willing, life-giving spirit of the Son of God that had been cultivated in Daniel.

Through the Triune-Light within this mature steward-son, God also *mentored* and greatly strengthened Daniel's three friends who would enter the fusion chamber and undergo the baptism of the fiery furnace:

> [Nebuchadnezzar said,] [25]"Look! I see four men loosed and walking about in the midst of the fire without harm, and the appearance of the fourth is like **a son of the gods!**" [*Nucleus of the Triune-God*]. [26]Then Nebuchadnezzar came near to the door of the furnace of blazing fire…and said, "Shadrach, Meshach and Abed-nego, come out, you **servants of the Most High God** [*fused into the Nucleus*], and come here!" (Dan. 3:25-26).

On several occasions, God miraculously and dramatically revealed Himself to Nebuchadnezzar, yet he had become so deeply acculturated into Worthless' nature and economy as the king of Babylon [*confusion*], each time he would gradually **regress into**

self-worth-ship and upward descent. Nevertheless, in *jealousy-for* him, God progressively *lifted* this distinguished dirt-bag *out* of Worthless' world and *into* the kingdom of God Most High. Nebuchadnezzar is a textbook example of the cosmic custody battle.

In a dream, God showed Nebuchadnezzar a beautiful, **mighty tree** in whose branches the inhabitants of the whole earth nested, but the tree (representing the king) was chopped down to a **stump** (see Dan. 4:15). Having built a mega-empire of dirt, Nebuchadnezzar congratulated and exalted himself. In reality, however, this king was just the unwitting pawn and captive that Worthless exploited to build *for himself* a **counterfeit of the true kingdom**. Jesus said, "The kingdom of heaven is like a mustard seed…and becomes **a tree**, so that birds of the air come and **nest in its branches**" (Matt. 13:31-32). As an ambassador of the Most High, Daniel was able to interpret the king's dream:

> [24]O king, this is the **decree of the Most High**, which has come upon my Lord the king: [25]that you be **driven away** [*exiled*] from mankind and **your dwelling place will be with the beasts of the field** [*dirt-dwellers*], and you will be given grass to eat like cattle…and seven periods of time will pass over you, until you **recognize that the Most High** [*three humble, selfless Eternals in mutual exaltation*] **is ruler** over

the realm of mankind....²⁶your kingdom will be assured to you after you recognize that it is **Heaven** [*the Triune-Dwelling Place*] **that rules** (Dan. 4:24-26).

Nebuchadnezzar *knew* Daniel was a son of God Most High; he *knew* this dream and interpretive warning was true, yet as a **compulsive lover of self**, addicted to "old wine [*desiring desire*]" (Luke 5:39), he was **eclipsed** and led astray by his own corrupt, inebriated spirit.

²⁹Twelve months later he was walking on the **roof** of the royal palace of Babylon [*e.g. pinnacle of con-fusion*]. ³⁰The king reflected and said, "Is this not Babylon the great, which **I myself have built** as a royal residence by the might of **my power** [*self-will*] and for the glory of **my majesty** [*self-worth-ship*]?" ³¹While the word was in the king's mouth, a voice came from heaven, saying, "King Nebuchadnezzar, to you it is declared: sovereignty has been removed from you...." ³³Immediately the word concerning Nebuchadnezzar [e.g. the law of upward descent] was fulfilled....

³⁴"But at the end of that period, I, Nebuchadnezzar, raised my eyes toward

heaven and my reason returned to me, and **I blessed the Most High** and praised and honored Him who lives forever...; His dominion is an everlasting [*unshakable*] dominion.... ³⁶My reason [*Agape rationale*] returned to me...so I was reestablished in my sovereignty [*as a steward-son*], and **surpassing greatness was added to me** [*downward ascent*]. ³⁷Now I, Nebuchadnezzar, praise, exalt and honor [*worth-ship*] the King of heaven [*e.g. I practice kingdom economics: reciprocal gene-rosity*], for all His works are **true** [*lit. truth; gen-uine*] and His ways **just** [*lit. justice; equality*], and **He is able to humble those who walk in pride**" (Dan. 4:29-37).

Paul: Caught Up To the Third Heaven

Before Paul was *re-gene-rated* into a *fuse-able* man, "**a man in Christ**...caught up to the third heaven" (2 Cor. 12:2), he was **Saul the Pharisee**—a self-righteous opportunist whose insatiable desire was to **promote himself** up the ranks of his religious sect by devouring those whom the Pharisees envied and hated: followers of Christ. "Saul began ravaging the church, entering house after house, and dragging off men and women, he would put them in prison" (Acts 8:3; see also Acts 9:1).

However, this **religious predator** was radically confronted by "**a light from heaven brighter than the sun** [*the Nucleus of the Trinity*]" (Acts 26:13) that literally knocked him off his donkey. "He **fell to the ground** [*in the dirt; upward descent*] and heard a voice saying, '…**I AM Jesus** who you are persecuting, but get up and enter the city, and it will be told to you **what you must do**'" (Acts 9:4-6). In other words, the Son of God Most High said, "You will no longer participate in the darkness of Worthless' religious economy; you work *for* Us now, and We will **mentor** you in kingdom economics." Saul's **re-education** and transformation into "Paul, a bond-servant of Christ Jesus" (Rom. 1:1) began with "the Light of the **knowledge** of the glory of God [*the fusion of the Trinity*] in the face of Christ [*the God-Man Nucleus*]" (2 Cor. 4:6).

The custody battle that the false-father wages against our true Father is particularly complex and cruel in religious circles. God's people are predestined to become sons and daughters of the Most High, yet they are often **sons of their own religious system** and therefore Worthless' sons (see John 8:44). In self-interest masked as spiritual fervor, these misguided sons jealously guard their own religious sect or denomination—a hierarchy that is grounded in Worthless' economy of hypocrisy and self-promotion. Among these religious captives, the false-father recruits agents of fission and mentors them as predatory opportunists. Jesus warned His followers, "They will make you **outcasts** from the synagogue [*disown you*], but an hour is coming for everyone who **kills you** [*seeks your death*] **to think** [*buy into Worthless' lie*] **that he is offering service to God** [*participating in God's economy*]" (John 16:2).

Saul was *born* into Worthless' religious world: *acculturated* into a religious form of individualism and self-worth-ship called **self-righteousness** and *mentored* by the deceiver in his religious marketplace as a zealous opportunist. In the Light of God in Christ, Saul was shocked and grieved to discover that he was actually being exploited by Worthless as a **double-agent**:

> [12]**I thank Christ Jesus** our Lord, who has strengthened me, because He considered me faithful [*full of faith*], **putting me into service** [*as a faith-full steward-son*], [13]even though I was formerly a blasphemer and a persecutor and a **violent aggressor** [*religious opportunist*]. Yet I was shown mercy because **I acted ignorantly in unbelief** [*I bought into Worthless' religious lie*] (1 Tim. 1:12-13).

Sustained exposure to the Light of the **knowledge** of God in Christ *penetrated* Saul's eclipse and progressively revealed that the very **rationale** assimilated into him while among the Pharisees over his lifetime actually had its source in the father of the lie. Not only had this self-referential thinking infected and corrupted his mind but it also his affections—

inflaming his insatiable desire and compelling him to behave as a religious predator. Jesus warned, "Beware of the **leaven** [*eros rationale*] **of the Pharisees,** which is hypocrisy [*the pretense of Agape with a hook*]" (Luke 12:1). This shocking discovery moved Saul to **exchange his own mind** for "the mind of Christ" (1 Cor. 2:19). He stated it a different way in chapter 10:

> [1]...by the **meekness and gentleness of Christ** [*by His gene-rous, life-giving DNA and Self-emptying example*]...[5]we are **destroying speculations** [*self-centered, eros rationale*] **and every lofty thing raised up against the knowledge of God** [*Most High: Three humble, childlike Eternals who exalt One Another*], and we are taking every [*self-referential*] thought captive to the **obedience of Christ** [*lose your life for My sake–fuse into the God-Man Nucleus*] (2 Cor. 10:1, 5).

As the Spirit cultivated the mind of Christ [*Agape rationale*] in Saul, he made a **comparative appraisal** of his own *worth* as a religious individualist with the *worth* of God in Christ: **"I do not consider** [*appraise*] **my life of any account as dear to myself** [*freedom from self-worth-ship*], so that I may finish my course and the **ministry** [*stewardship*] I received from the Lord Jesus, to testify solemnly of the **gospel** of the grace of God [*e.g. extend Jesus' invitation to participate in the Triune-Most High in and through Him*]" (Acts 20:24).

In order to **buy into** the fullness of the kingdom of God in Christ by sacrificial **self-giving**, Saul tore down, dismantled, and **sold** the empire of dirt he had labored so hard to build for himself in Worthless' religious world by **self-promotion**.

> [13]...but one thing I do: forgetting what lies behind [*my own life, achievements, and identity as a religious individualist in Worthless' marketplace*], and reaching forward to what lies ahead, [14]**I press on** [*emigrating*] **toward the goal for the prize** [*true riches, inheritance*] **of the upward call of God** [*Most High*] **in Christ Jesus** [*the kingdom: fusion of God and man in the God-Man Nucleus*]. [16]...let us keep living by that same **standard** [*seek first His interests in one another*] to which we have attained [*maintaining the same Agape*]. [17]Brethren, join in following **my example** [*individually: a life-giving spirit, a fuse-able man*], and observe those who walk according to **the pattern** [*relational blueprints*] **you have in us** [*corporately: self-giving individuals practicing reciprocal gene-rosity and maturing together in Trinity-likeness*] (Phil. 3:13-17).

As a Pharisee, Saul was very familiar with offering God temple sacrifices of animals and produce, but the whole system of worth-ship had long been **corrupted** by *eros* **payoffs**. The very meeting place provided for the people to practice reciprocal giving with God had become Worthless' marketplace; Jesus described the Temple as "a place of business" (John 2:16) and "**a robbers' den**" (Matt. 21:13). However, Saul discovered that *in* and *through* the Nucleus of Christ, a new and living way was provided for us to truly know the Triune-God of *Agape* and reciprocate Their *generosity*, not by sacrificing sheep and doves and grain but by **sacrificing *self***: "Present your bodies a **living and holy** [*eros-free*] **sacrifice, acceptable to God** [*Three sacrificial Self-givers*], which is your spiritual service of worship [*worth-ship*]" (Rom. 12:1). Paul exhorted his son Timothy to **"...discipline yourself** [*practice self-denial and self-giving*] for the purpose of **godliness** [*Trinity-like fusion*]; ....godliness is **profitable for all things** [*natural and spiritual bounty*], since it holds promise for the **present life** and also for the life to come" (1 Tim. 4:7-8).

Exposure to the extreme self-forsaking Love, which Father, Son, and Spirit *are*, moved **Saul** to *willingly lose* his life as a **religious opportunist**. Therefore, he awakened to *find* his life as a new, fuse-able creation named **Paul**, who said, "I have been crucified with Christ; and it is no longer I [*Saul*] who live, but **Christ lives in me** [*Paul, a bondservant of Christ*]" (Gal. 2:20). Paul not only **sold** all his achievements and aspirations in Worthless' religious world to **buy** into the God-Man Nucleus, he also **exchanged** his own racial, tribal, and vocational identity in order to become, simply, "**a man in Christ**" (2 Cor. 12:2). He wrote, "Christ will even now, as always, be **exalted** [*worth-shipped*] **in my body**, whether by life or by death" (Phil. 1:20).

As the Spirit actively *re-gene-rated* Paul—maturing *within* him Christ's own nature—Paul *practiced* reciprocal gene-rosity in the economy of the kingdom and was moved from within to *seek first His*. Paul's own desire was transformed into a powerful, inward compulsion **to embody and fulfill Christ's desire**. The more Paul became *acculturated* into the relational, inter-personal life of the Triune-Most High— *downward ascent*—the deeper he saw into the very *gene-rative* Source of the superabundant bounty of the kingdom: the humble, **Self-forgetful** nature of Father, Son, and Spirit, which was revealed in and through the life and death of the God-Man Jesus. Paul was certainly no longer Saul, the self-promoting Pharisee, but as a son of the Most High, neither did he cherish his own individuality as "Paul." Rather, he declared, "**I am a nobody**" (2 Cor. 12:11). This *nobody*, this self-emptied individual, this *self-forgetful* man fused into Christ, was **made ready to be lifted** further into the relational fullness of the Most High. In fact, Paul could not even describe his own experience of the third heaven in the first person:

> [2]I know **a man in Christ** [*effectively fused into the God-Man Nucleus*] who fourteen years ago—whether in the body [*dirt-*

bag] I do not know, or out of the body I do not know, God knows—**such a man** [*made fuse-able*] **was caught up to the third heaven** [*mutual indwelling place of Father, Son, and Spirit*]. [4]...caught up into **Paradise** [*bountiful economy of three Self-sharers*] (2 Cor. 12:2-4).

The Triune-Most High *lifted* Paul into Themselves for these purposes: to naturalize and acculturate him in Their kind of Self-emptying, Self-forgetful *generosity*; to fill him with Their relational fullness as a steward-son; to mature him as an ambassador of "the Love of God, which is in Christ Jesus" (Rom. 8:39); and to enlarge him as a conduit through whom They could pour out Their fullness on the earth. Paul said, "**I am being poured out as a drink offering** upon the sacrifice and service of *your* faith" (Phil. 2:17).

There is a vast difference between being a giving sort of person versus **emptying** your whole person so that Christ Jesus can inhabit you, fill you, and express *the fullness* of His own gene-rosity through you to others. Paul was not simply a giving man, he became a living temple inhabited by Another. Out from this consecrated and filled dirt-bag, Christ continued to pour the fullness of the Trinity into the world. Therefore, the economy of the kingdom of the Triune-Most High was **embodied** within Paul. As a bond-servant of Christ Jesus, Paul said, "I am **under obligation** [*lit. a debtor; e.g. of Agape*] both to Greeks and to barbarians, both to the wise and to the foolish" (Rom. 1:14).

It is often said, "It takes one to know one"; the more Paul *matured* as a steward-son, the more he *cherished* the magnitude of the Son's Self-giving: "though He was **rich**, yet for your sake He became **poor**, so that you through His **poverty** [*comprehensive Self-expenditure*] might become **rich**" (2 Cor. 8:9). See Paul's own testimony as a son inhabited by Christ: "...as **dying** [*to self*] yet behold we **live** [*in fusion Oneness*]...as **poor** yet making many **rich**, as **having nothing** [*exchanging proprietorship for stewardship*] yet **possessing all things** [*sons and heirs of God Most High*]" (2 Cor. 6:9-10).

Paul grew to understand and act upon Jesus' words, "Blessed are the **poor in spirit** [*self-emptied, self-forgetful*], for theirs is the **kingdom** of heaven [*the relational fullness of the Triune-God in Christ*]" (Matt. 5:3). According to *downward ascent*, the more Paul **emptied** himself, allowing the Triune-God to pour out Their superabundant "fullness" to others *through* his *gene-rosity*, the more he himself **inherited** the kingdom of the three sacrificial Self-sharers whom He served! "I will not be a burden to you [*e.g. I have come as a burden-bearer*]; for **I do not seek what is yours** [*as an opportunist*], **but you** [*God's treasured inheritance, therefore mine*].... I will most gladly **spend and be expended for your souls** [*kingdom economics*] (2 Cor. 12:14-15).

See how far *downward ascent* actually goes. Jürgen Moltmann observed that *Agape* humiliates itself for the sake of its beloved.[7] In Christ, Father, Son, and Spirit **humiliated** Themselves before Their beloved, "the world" (John 3:16) as a necessary antidote for our **self-exaltation** as *eros*-infected captives of the lie. The cross teaches us that embracing humiliation is a mature form of sacrificial self-giving Love that effectively *exposes* self-worth-ship, *disarms* individualism, and *overcomes* self-exaltation. Without conquering our pride by embracing humiliation, the Triune-Most High could not *lift* us into Themselves. Father, Son, and Spirit *are* God Most High *because* of Their humility and mutual exaltation. **Embracing the humiliation** of coming to us "in the likeness of sinful flesh [*incarnated into a dirt-bag*]" (Rom. 8:3) and embracing the cross for our sakes was the supreme manifestation of **God's glory!**

As a *gen-uine* son of the Most High, Paul practiced this advanced form of kingdom economics: "**humbling myself so that *you* may be exalted**" (2 Cor. 11:7). From personal experience, Paul knew the only thing powerful enough to *conquer* the arrogance of self-righteousness and self-promotion is extreme self-forsaking Love; therefore, Paul willingly allowed the Spirit of Christ prevailing within him to continue providing this antidote to arrogant men through *his own* humiliation:

---

[7] Moltmann, J. (1981). *The Trinity and the Kingdom.* Augsberg Fortress Publishers.

²⁰**I am afraid that** perhaps when I come I may find you to be not what I wish [*arrogant, self-exalting*] and may be found by you to be not what you wish [*resenting the spiritual authority of Christ within me*]; that perhaps there will be [*fission:*] **strife**, **jealousy**, angry tempers, disputes, slanders, gossip, **arrogance**, disturbances; ²¹I am afraid that when I come again **my God may humiliate me before you** [*as a necessary antidote to your self-exaltation*]… (2 Cor. 12:20-21).

Two Economies in Head-On Collision

Nothing helps us to distinguish the economy of Worthless' world from the economy of the kingdom quite like seeing them violently collide. Turbulent upheavals occur when the *inverted vortex* of upward descent encounters the *life-giving Vortex* of downward ascent! In *the twelve stages of relational fission*, we already examined the most intense example of this conflict— how Satan, the opportunist, gained a foothold in Judas and compelled him to betray Jesus for thirty pieces of silver, but see the prelude to the story:

> ³Mary then took a pound of **very costly perfume** of pure nard, and anointed the feet of Jesus [*reciprocal gene-rosity*] and wiped his feet with her hair [*downward ascent*]; and the house was **filled** with

the fragrance of the perfume [*fullness of relational fusion*]. ⁴But Judas Iscariot... who was intending to betray Him, said, ⁵"Why was this perfume not **sold for three hundred denarii** and given to poor people?" ⁶Now he said this, not because he was concerned about the poor, but because he was a **thief**... (John 12:3-6).

Matthew also recorded this particular confrontation: "But the disciples were **indignant** when they saw this, and said, '**Why this waste?**' ...But Jesus, aware of this, said to them, 'Why do you bother the woman [*pull her down in your crab bucket*]? For she has done **a good deed** to Me [*reciprocal gene-rosity*]'" (Matt. 26:8-10). Recognizing and following the way of *downward ascent*, Mary became acculturated into God's economy of worth long before the disciples who were still moving in *upward descent*: en route to Jerusalem, "there arose a dispute among them as to which one [*individualist*] of them was regarded to be greatest" (Luke 22:24). Though Judas was a thief, *all* of the disciples were still inebriated addicts of self-worth-ship.

Once the Spirit opens your eyes to *kingdom economics*, you will discover the Scriptures are *filled* with these head-on collisions such as **Ananias and Sapphira's financial contribution,** which was a *fatal* lie (see Acts 5:1-5), but we will look briefly at two others: Jesus cleansing the temple and the riot which Paul precipitated in Ephesus over the goddess Artemis.

> [12]Jesus entered **the temple** [*center established to practice kingdom economics: reciprocal gene-rosity*] and **drove out** all those who were **buying and selling** in the temple, and overturned the tables of the money changers [*opportunists practicing Worthless' economics*] and the seats of those who were **selling doves** [*symbol of the peace which sacrificial self-givers share in one Spirit*]. [13]And He said to them, "It is written, 'My house [*cohabitation*] shall be called a **house of prayer** [*communion, relational fusion, mutual indwelling, perichoresis*]'; but you are making it a **robbers' den** [*marketplace of predators*]" (Matt. 21:12-13).

Jesus, Son of the Most High God" **embodied** *within Himself* the economy of the kingdom and its fullness. Wherever Jesus went, this transcendent economy **invaded** Worthless' secular and religious marketplace and **confronted** the corrupt dirt-bags sitting in it. Consider Zaccheus' encounter with Jesus (see Luke 19:1-10). Since mammon [*desiring desire*] is one of the primary ways the false-father wages his custody battle, this invasion was often violent. John also witnessed Jesus cleansing the temple:

¹⁴And He found in the temple those who were **selling** oxen and sheep and doves, and the **money changers** seated at their tables. ¹⁵And He made a scourge of cords, and **drove** [*whipped*] **them all out** of the temple… and He **poured out** the coins of the **money changers** and **overturned** their tables; ¹⁶and to those who were **selling the doves** He said, "Take these things away; **stop making My Father's house a place of business** [*Worthless' marketplace*]." ¹⁷His disciples remembered that it was written, "**Zeal** [*jealousy*] **for Your house** [*fusion cohabitation*] **will consume me** [*move Me to willingly forfeit my own life*]" (John 2:14-17).

"Our God is a **consuming fire**" (Heb. 12:29). This fire is the **zealous, jealous-for Love** [*Agape*] of Father, Son, and Spirit *for* One Another and *for* us. The Steward-Son is *jealous-for* the sacred nest of vulnerable rest that Father, Spirit, and you and me are destined to share in reciprocal gene-rosity *in Him*. Therefore, Jesus whipped and kicked the agents of Worthless' economy out of the temple. The fire of God in Christ desperately wants to consume the lie—**burn Worthless' corrupt economic practices out of us**—so that we as living stones might become an *eros*-free cohabitation for the Triune-God and one another. In a brilliant message entitled "**Merchandising Truth**," Meister Eckhart made this pointed observation:

But who, exactly, are the people that **buy and sell**? Are they not precisely the **good people**? See! The merchants are those who only guard against moral sins. They strive to be good people who do their good deeds to the glory of God, such as fasting, watching, praying and the like—all of which are good—and yet do these things so that God will give them something in **exchange**. Their efforts are contingent upon God doing something they ardently want to have done [*eros payoff*].

They are all merchants [*religious opportunists*]. They want to exchange one thing for another and to trade with our Lord. But they will be **cheated out of their bargain** [*by the law of upward descent*]— for what they have or have attained is actually **given** to them by God. Lest we forget, we do what we do only by the help of God, and so **God is never obligated to us**. God gives us nothing except out of His own free will. What we are we are because of God, and whatever we have we receive from God and not by our own **contriving** [*eros calculation, opportunism*]. Therefore God is not in the least obligated to us—neither for our deeds nor for our gifts. **He gives to us freely**....

People are very foolish when they want to **trade** with God. They know little or nothing of **the truth** [*reciprocal, sacrificial self-giving; downward ascent*]. And God will strike them and drive them out of the temple. Light and darkness cannot exist side by side. God Himself is the truth [*true Triune-Love*]. When He [*God in Christ*] enters the temple, **he drives out ignorance and darkness** and reveals Himself in light and truth. Then, when the truth is known, **merchants must depart—for truth wants no merchandising!** God does not seek His own benefit. In everything He acts only out of love [*Agape*]. Thus, the person who is united [*fused*] with God lives the same way [*kingdom economics*]— he is innocent and free [*eros-free*]. He lives for love without asking why, and solely for the glory of God, never seeking his own advantage. God alone is at work in Him ["the truth of Christ is in me" 2 Cor. 11:10]....

If you want to be rid of the **commercial spirit**, then by all means do all you can in the way of good works, but do so solely for the praise of God. **Live as if you did not exist** [*self-forgetful; "I am a nobody"*]. Expect and ask nothing in return. Then

the merchant [*opportunist*] **inside of you will be driven out** of the temple God has made. Then God alone dwells there. See! This is how the temple is cleared: when a person thinks only of God [*seeks first His*] and honors Him alone [*true worth-ship*]. Only such a person is free and **genuine.**[8]

The **riot at Ephesus** is the second example of these two, opposite economies in a head-on collision. Paul testified, "In holiness and **godly sincerity** [*Trinity-like gene-rosity without hypocrisy*], not in **fleshly wisdom** [*eros rationale: calculation and opportunism*] but in the grace of God, we have **conducted ourselves in the world** [*counter-culture in Worthless' marketplace*]" (2 Cor. 1:12). As a mature steward-son of the Most High, Paul **embodied** the economy of the kingdom; everywhere he went, some bought into this inheritance and began practicing reciprocal gene-rosity, while others who were deeply invested in Worthless' world economy reacted violently to his presence and spiritual authority. Jesus said, "Do not think that I came to bring **peace** on the earth [*e.g. tolerance for Worthless' economic tyranny*]; I did not come to bring peace, **but a sword** [*"to destroy the works of the devil" 1 John 3:8*]" (Matt. 10:34). Paul and those in Ephesus who bought into **the Way** of the kingdom inadvertently provoked the captives of Worthless' religious marketplace:

[8] Eckhart, Meister. (2003). *The Bread and the Wine.* "Merchandising Truth," Plough Publishing House, p. 107.

[23]…there occurred no small disturbance concerning **the Way** [*sons of the Most High practicing kingdom economics*]. [24]For a man named Demetrius, a **silversmith** [*slave of mammon*], who made silver shrines of Artemis, was bringing **no little business** to the craftsmen; [25]these he gathered together with the workmen of similar trades [*opportunists in con-fusion*], and said, "Men, you know that **our prosperity depends upon this business.** [26]…Paul has persuaded and turned away a considerable number of people, saying that gods made with hands are no gods at all. [27]Not only is there danger that **this trade of ours fall into disrepute**, but also that the temple of the great goddess Artemis be regarded as **worthless** and that she whom all of Asia and the world worship will even be **dethroned from her magnificence** [*upward descent*]."

[28]When they heard this they were **filled with rage**, they began crying out, saying, "Great is Artemis of the Ephesians!" [29]The city was **filled with confusion**, and they rushed with **one accord** [*counterfeit fusion*] into the theater. [34]…a **single outcry** arose from them all as they shouted for about two hours, "Great is Artemis of the

Ephesians!" [35]After quieting the crowd, the town clerk said, "Men of Ephesus, what man is there after all who does not know that the city of the Ephesians is the **guardian** of the temple of the great Artemis and of **the image which fell down from heaven**?" (Acts 19:23-35).

Satan chose the façade of Artemis as his own self-image among the Ephesians to exploit their worship. These men bought into Worthless' lie and became the captive work-force by which he built for himself a mighty, self-exalting city with a sophisticated economic system. Upon the pinnacle of this counterfeit cohabitation Worthless sat enthroned as its figurehead in disguise. Curiously, Artemis is a female deity, who captivates men by sensual allurement—a customized snare unique to the insatiable desire and corrupt self-image of these particular people. In Europe she is Europa riding on the beast; in India she is Cali and other gods shrewdly crafted by Worthless. Men worth-ship her in *eros*, believing they will get both a sexual and financial payoff and become the influential men they imagine themselves to be. When disturbed, their jealous rage is not really for her but for self. This system, which the false-father replicates in every place on earth, actually works for a time since these inebriated, dispirited dirt-bags do not realize they are being exploited as slaves by chasing Worthless' mirage.

Understanding the dynamic of these two conflicting economies greatly illumines Jesus' words:

²⁰Blessed are you who are **poor** [*in Worthless' world economy*], for yours is the kingdom of God [*the superabundant "fullness" of reciprocal gene-rosity with the Triune-Most High*]. ²²**...Blessed are you when men hate you**, and ostracize you, and insult you, and scorn your name as evil, for the sake of the Son of Man [*men confronted by the Nucleus of the economy of the kingdom embodied within you*]. ²³Be glad in that day and leap for joy, for behold, your **reward** is great in heaven [*downward ascent*].... ²⁴But woe to you who are **rich** [*by insatiable desire, opportunism, and confusion*], for you are receiving your comfort in full [*upward descent*]... ²⁶**Woe to you when all men speak well of you** [*e.g. if your presence in Worthless' marketplace provokes no confrontation from its captives, you yourself are one of them!*]... (Luke 6:20-26).

The Light of the economy of the kingdom within sons and daughters of the Most High seriously threatens and provokes men who have *sold themselves* into Worthless' counterfeit economic system. If these **head-on collisions** do not happen in your sphere of influence, then you are not yet practicing kingdom economics in a Trinity-like way or **carrying that transcendent authority within you**. "The people who know their God [*sons and daughters of the Most High*] shall prove themselves strong and shall stand firm and do exploits [*overcome and destroy Worthless' economic tyranny*] [for God]." (Dan. 11:32 AMP). T. Austin Sparks explains our stewarded authority:

After the Cross, all the **fulness** of the Divine power was **released** upon the world through those [*sons and daughters*] who had been brought into **absolute oneness** [*gen-uine fusion*] with the Lord by that Cross. That is the peculiar kind of **knowledge** [*wisdom from above: Son and Nucleus of the Triune-Most High*] which means the **release of such forces and such powers upon the world situation** [*engaging predators in a famine*] as are unknown by the great **world systems** [*Worthless' eclipsed marketplaces*].

...What does our personal presence in a situation mean? [*Is the economy of the kingdom embodied within us?*] Does it mean that there is the going out of a **power** [*downward ascent*] which cannot be **accounted** for on any human basis whatever [*in Worthless' rationale and economy: upward descent*], but which is a **greater** [*overcoming, fusion*] **force** than the forces [*of fission, con-fusion*] that are represented by **world organizations**, **world methods, world resources?**[9]

Emigrating into God Most High

The Son Jesus is **the Nucleus** of all the fullness of the Triune-God. Jesus said, "I AM **the Way** and **the Truth** and **the Life**" (John 14:6). **The Way** Father, Son, and Spirit, as Individuals, *debit* Self to *credit* One Another is the bountiful economy of the kingdom of God. According to *relational altruism*—the Truth—these three sacrificial Self-givers willingly and perpetually *fuse into* One Another as one "incorruptible God" (Rom. 1:23). **The Life,** which Father, Son, and Spirit *share* in fusion Oneness, facilitates a relational, inter-Personal infrastructure—a *mutual-indwelling place*—known as the kingdom of God. According to "**the Way** and **the Truth** and **the Life**," these Three humble, *Self-less* Eternals constantly *exalt* One Another, therefore moving together in downward ascent, they "dwell on a high and holy place" (Isa. 57:15) as **God Most High**.

The **eternal Son** of the Most High was incarnated into human flesh as the Man Jesus in order to become our "**Forerunner**" (Heb. 6:20). For the sake of us *de-gene-rate* dirt-bags who *bought into* the lie of individualism and *fell* into self-worth-ship, this God-Man came to **blaze a trail** back into God Most High.

[9] Sparks, T. Austin. (n.d.). *Vision and Vocation.* "The People That Do Exploits." Retrieved from http://www.austin-sparks.net/english/books/001535.html.

The Son Jesus *became* the Way by practicing kingdom economics as a Man—rediscovering and treasuring the cohabitation of heaven, *buying into* it by sacrificial Self-giving, and maturing in *reciprocal gene-rosity* with Father and Spirit as **a tested**, **perfected**, ***human* Son**. The Son Jesus sacrificially *emptied* Himself in order to *receive* into Himself, as a *human* Nucleus, **all the fullness** of the superabundant life of the Triune-Most High.

In the first century, followers of Jesus were literally called "**the Way**" (Acts 9:2; 19:9, 23) because they intentionally and progressively **relocated** the investment of themselves *out* of Worthless' world economy and *into* the economy of the kingdom according to *the Way* Jesus, their economic advisor, modeled for them:

> [31]If you **continue in My word** [*emigrating into God Most High by practicing kingdom economics*], then you are **truly** [*gen-uinely*] **disciples of Mine** [*followers of "the Way": downward ascent*]; [32]and you will know **the truth** [*the Light of the knowledge Triune-Agape*], and **the truth will make you free** [*from desiring desire, self-worthship, individualism*]. [36]....If the Son [*our perfected Forerunner and Nucleus*] makes you **free** [*from the tyranny of Worthless' nature, rationale, and labor-camp*], you will be **free indeed** [*to participate as self-sharers*

in "the life" of God Most High] (John 8:31-32, 36).

Paul referred to God's Own Way of *downward ascent*, which Jesus embodied and *personified*, as "**the upward call of God in Christ Jesus**" (Phil. 3:14). Through the Way:

> [3]O send out Your **light** and Your **truth** [*Jesus, Son and Nucleus of the Triune-God*], and let them **lead me**; let them **bring me** [*by downward ascent*] to Your holy hill and to Your dwelling places [*into God Most High*]. [4]Then **I will go** [*as a willing, living sacrifice*] **to the altar** [*into the fusion chamber*] **of God,** to God my exceeding joy [*inheritance of life*]… (Ps. 43:3-4).

We are called to **emigrate** *out* of Worthless' world and *into* the kingdom of God Most High by practicing kingdom economics individually and together according to "*the Way*." Jeremiah prophesied:

> [19]…**To You** [*Son and Nucleus of God Most High*] **the nations will come** [*emigrate*] **from the ends of the earth** [*out of Worthless' world*] and say, "Our fathers have **inherited** nothing but **falsehood** [*de-gene-rate, eros heredity: the lie*], **futility** [*Worthless' corrupt economy*] and things of **no profit** [*mirages leading to famine: upward descent*]." [20]Can

a man **make gods for himself** [*laboring in self-worth-ship*]? Yet they are not gods [*counterfeits*]! [21]Therefore behold, I am going to make them **know** [*incorruptible truth: kingdom economics*]—this time I will make them **know My power** and My might [*Jesus, the God-Man Nucleus: Source of the superabundant, gene-rative Life of the All-Three-Mighty*]... (Jer. 16:19-21).

The Apostle John taught us how to discern the truth from the lie (1 John 4:6). But, due to the **emigrant journey** Paul made *out* of the darkness of religious hypocrisy, he has the most to teach us about *emigrating* into God Most High:

[1]And you were **dead** [*dispirited, cast down, fallen*] in your trespasses and sins, [2]in which **you formerly walked according to** [*acculturated into*] **the course of this world** [*upward descent: buying and selling one another in Worthless' marketplace*], according to the prince of the power of the air [*fallen archangel: "another great eagle" Ezek. 17:7–an imposter, the father of the lie*], of **the spirit** [*self-worth-ship*] **that is working** [*maturing*] **in the sons of disobedience** [*mentored as predatory opportunists by the false-father*]. [3]Among them we too all formerly lived [*in confusion*] in the lusts of our flesh, **indulging**

the desires of the flesh [*desiring desire*] **and of the mind** [*eros rationale*], and were by nature children of wrath, even as the rest.

[4]But God, being **rich** in mercy, because of His great **Agape** with which He loved us [*bountiful yield of Triune-Agape: "fullness" poured out on us*], [5]even when we were **dead** in our transgressions [the living dead: flesh-eating zombies], made us **alive** together with Christ [*Man perfected in reciprocal gene-rosity*] [6]…and **raised us up with Him** [*into the Triune-Most High*], and seated us with Him [*in relational rest*] in the heavenly places **in Christ Jesus** [*God-Man Nucleus of our cohabitation*], [7]so that in the ages to come He might show the surpassing **riches** of His grace in kindness toward us [*Three Self-sharers sharing Their superabundant life with us*] **in Christ Jesus** (Eph. 2:1-7).

Sadly, most of us believers are still so anxious about our material provision, inebriated by self-focus and shopping for dirt in Worthless' marketplace that we do not even realize we are in Christ and that **we are already seated with Him in God Most High**! The fullness of the kingdom has *already* been given to us: in Christ, you have been made full and complete (see

Col. 2:10). Father and Son have already given us the Spirit as a down payment of our inheritance (see Eph. 1:14), and *through* the eternal Spirit *all* the fullnesses of the Triune-Most High is *already* opened to us and waiting to be entered and explored! "Because you are sons, God has **sent forth the Spirit** of His **Son** into our hearts, crying, 'Abba! **Father!**'" (Gal. 4:6). We as half-formed sons and daughters must now continue **emigrating** into the Triune-Most High by the Way of *downward ascent* and become **acculturated** into Their abundant life by *sharing* in Their economy. Paul testified of this **spiritual awakening**:

> ...we [*emigrants*] do not look at [*focus on, appraise, cherish*] the things which are **seen** [*dirt: self-focus, flesh, materialism*], but at the things which are **not seen** [*transcendent Reality: spiritual cohabitation of God Most High*]; for the things which are seen are **temporal** [*decaying in corruption: fissionable, shakable*], but the things which are not seen are **eternal** [incorruptible, unshakable] (2 Cor. 4:18).

Our emigrant journey is "from faith to faith" (Rom. 1:17) and "from life to life" (2 Cor. 2:16) and "from glory to glory" (2 Cor. 3:18). How does this work? "The **path** of the righteous [*emigrants who practice kingdom economics according to "the Way"*] is like the light of dawn that shines **brighter and brighter until the full day**" (Prov. 4:18). We are already *in* the light of dawn, yet we must *journey* into the full day. The further we progress into the fullnesses of the kingdom, the more our eclipse recedes, and our economy of values (worth-ship) is adjusted accordingly. We find ourselves constantly cashing out our treasured investments in this world and relocating them above. Paul described this emigrant journey:

> ¹Therefore, if you have been **raised up** with Christ [*out of Worthless' world and into God Most High*], **keep seeking the things above** [*emigrating into your inheritance by practicing kingdom economics*], where Christ [*our Forerunner Man*] is, seated at the right hand of God. ²Set your **minds on the things above** [*Agape rationale: appraising "true riches" as relational fullnesses in fusion Oneness*], not on the things that are on **earth** [*eros rationale: cherishing dirt–materialism, self-indulgence, the flesh*]. ³For you have **died** [*to desiring desire itself for self*] and **your life is hidden with Christ in God** [*fused into the Nucleus: Rock of Triune-Solidarity*]. ⁴When Christ, who is **our life** [*God-Man in whom and through whom we participate in the fusion of the Trinity*], **is revealed** [*second coming*], then you also will be **revealed with Him in glory** [*perfected in the relational Oneness you have practiced together as "imitators" of the Triune-Most High*] (Col. 3:1-4).

How do we *seek the things above?* How do we emigrate? Each individual believer receives a call to become an emigrant to the kingdom, but he cannot get very far by himself! Individuals must emigrate *together* into the Triune-Most High "by being of the **same mind** [*Agape rationale*], maintaining the **same Agape** [*cleaving to one another*], **united in spirit** [*individual "life-giving spirits" in fusion*], **intent on one purpose** [*to "seek first His" together*]" (Phil. 2:2). Paul provided us fellow-emigrants with a mandate:

> [1]Therefore, be **imitators of God** [*Father, Son, and Spirit*], as beloved children; [2]and **walk in Agape** [*emigrate to the kingdom by practicing Trinity-likeness*], **just as Christ** [*our Forerunner, the Way*] also loved you and gave Himself up for us [*redeemed us with the currency of sacrificial Self-giving*], an offering and a sacrifice to God [*to re-gene-rate us as sons and daughters of the Most High*]… (Eph. 5:1-2).

Imitators of God are individual believers who **practice Trinity-likeness together**. Paul told us how: "Let *Agape* be without hypocrisy [*the lie*]….Be **devoted** to one another in brotherly love [*bearing one another's burdens*], **give preference** to one another in honor [*lit. Greek: **outdo one another in showing honor**; e.g. even as Father, Son, and Spirit mutually exalt One Another*]" (Rom. 12:9-10). As emigrants, we are *not* trying to get to heaven; rather, we are seeking to be *fused* into the relational, inter-personal infrastructure of the kingdom of God. Our Forerunner Jesus clearly mapped out our **destination**: "that they [*individual believers*] may all be one [*fused*], even as We are one [*Triune-God*]; even as You Father are in Me and I in You [*relational fusion*], **that they may also be in Us** [*lifted into God Most High*]…" (John 17:21).

Stated simply, we fellow-emigrants are *lifted* into the Triune-Most High according to the measure we have learned to *lift one another* in mutual exaltation— "**the building up of one another** [*Trinity-likeness*]" (Rom. 14:19). Jude urged, "**Keep yourselves** [*together*] **in the** *Agape* **of God**" (Jude 21). *The Message* translates it this way: "Stay right at the center [*Nucleus*] of God's *Agape.*" We are *already* in the God-Man Nucleus, but can we learn to abide in Him *together* by **practicing** the Way and the Truth and the Life with one another in a Trinity-like way? A lifetime emigrant journey is required to cover the distance between *individual* Christianity (my personal "faith") to a *corporate* expression of the kingdom—"one body…one faith… one baptism…one mind…one purpose" (Eph. 4:4-6; Phil. 1:27)!

What, exactly, would it look like for us, as *imitators of God*, to be **one** even as Father, Son, and Spirit are **one**? The Scriptures describe sons and daughters who have *matured* together in Trinity-likeness as a **many-membered bride**—a suitable counterpart for our **Triune-Groom**—a heavenly people, the "church of God in [*fused into*] Christ Jesus" (1 Thes. 2:14). The Triune-Groom has desired this many-membered bride from the very beginning: "Then God said, 'Let **Us** [*Father, Son, Spirit*] make man in **Our image**, according to **Our likeness**'" (Gen. 1:26).

The kingdom of our Triune-God is an **abundant relational life** (see John 10:10; 2 Pet. 1:11)—an infinite progression of relational fullnesses that can only be discovered and entered by those who practice *reciprocal gene-rosity* with one another. Paul wrote, "Your faith is greatly **enlarged** and the *Agape* of each one of you toward one another **grows** ever greater....May the Lord [*Father, Son, Spirit*] cause you to **increase and abound in *Agape* for one another**" (1 Thes. 1:3; 3:12). The kingdom of God is also a **reciprocal inheritance**. Our Triune-Groom eagerly waits to *inherit* one many-membered bride comprised of fuse-able individuals who give, receive, and cherish *one another* just as Father, Son, and Spirit cherish One Another. Paul wrote to believers in Thessalonica:

> 2:19For who is our hope or joy or **crown of exultation**? Is it not even you, in the presence of our Lord Jesus [*our Nucleus*]...? 20For you are our **glory** and joy [*our inheritance*]. 3:9For what thanks can we **render to God for you in return** [*reciprocal gene-rosity*] for all the joy with which we rejoice before our God on **your account...**?" (1 Thes. 2:19-20; 3:9).

As we believers emigrate together into the kingdom, which Father already opened to us in the Son through the Spirit, we are **exposed to the glory of our Triune-Groom** and we are moved to *worthship* Him by practicing Trinity-likeness together. As we become one another's cherished inheritance in reciprocal gene-rosity, our Triune-Groom begins to inherit us as one bride prepared as Their suitable counterpart—a fused and fuse-able DNA-match! John addressed this *re-gene-rating* bride as **one devoted and responsive "lady"** (2 John 1-8). As a many-membered bride, we must empty ourselves of individualism and self-exaltation and humbly seek first the interests of our Triune-Groom together: "Exalt the Lord our God and worship at His footstool [*sacrificially give ourselves together in downward ascent*]; Holy is He [*"Holy, Holy, Holy" fused in incorruptible Oneness*]" (Ps. 99:5).

Our minds, affections, conversation, energies, and resources should be **centered** upon Father, Son, and Spirit—what They are presently saying and doing and how *together* we can sacrificially *give* ourselves to be **the embodiment** and expression of Their kingdom on earth as it is in heaven. Ultimately, it is one, prepared, many-membered bride, who is *lifted* into the household of God Most High because she has been made ready to fuse into her Triune-Groom.

As a fitting conclusion, T. Austin Sparks described in economic terms what it means for us to be called up into God Most High as **a heavenly people**:

Christ [*the Nucleus of the Triune-Most High*] **is a heavenly revelation**, but Christ is also a **heavenly fullness**. If God has revealed His mind, His thought in Christ [*the way, the truth, the life*]; if all that God intended has been brought to us in a Personal revelation, God has followed that up by the **fullest provision** in Christ for its realization and its attainment. So that **every need of ours** [*to prepare ourselves as a fused and fuse-able bride*] **is supplied according to His riches in glory** [*bounty*] in Christ Jesus. In Christ [*our all-true Forerunner*] there is not only a standard set [*the law of reciprocal Agape*], but every kind of provision for attaining to God's standard. All the **secret resources** of God to reach His end [*fusion of God and man in the God-Man*] are there in Christ for us.... All the **fullness** dwells in Him [*Nucleus of the Trinity*], and we are **made full** in Him (Col. 2:9)....

God's thought is centered in Christ in heaven, and **God's resources are centered in Christ in heaven** [*accessed by our life-giving spirit fused into the Spirit of Christ*]. That means that the Lord's people in this dispensation are essentially a heavenly people, and that means it is quite **impossible to attain unto God's thought or to know God's resources in Christ until we are a heavenly people** [*a Trinity-like us: sons and daughters of God Most High who lift and carry one another in downward ascent*]. If in any way or in any measure we are **earthbound** [individualists fixated on dirt], it will be in that measure impossible to attain unto God's thought, and to know God's **resources** [*kingdom bounty*].

God only takes responsibility to supply and to carry on that which is essentially **heavenly** [*emigrants practicing kingdom economics together*], and in the measure in which a thing is heavenly, and only in that measure (but surely in that measure), **God takes responsibility for it** [*Father knows… feeds… clothes*]. If it is in any way **linked with this world** [*con-fused into Worthless' world economy*], becoming a part of this **world system** [*self-worth-ship: upward descent*], related to this **earth** [*an empire of dirt*], it has got to take responsibility for itself to carry its own weight, to find its own resources [*amidst famine*], to see its own way through.[10]

---

[10] Sparks, T. (n.d.) *That Which Was From The Beginning*, Chapter 1 – "God's Beginning Govern's His End" Retrieved from http://www.austin-sparks.net/english/books/that_which_was_from_the_beginning.html).

God Magnified Series

Part 1: Discovering the "Us" in Oneness

A journey of progressive magnification of the worth-ship of God by meditating on five of the fourteen "God is" statements in Scripture. These statements are like porch pillars of the eternal dwelling place that the Trinity share in perpetual fusion Oneness in *Agape*. The Triune-God intentionally left Their spiritual fingerprint in the powersource of the natural universe—atomic nuclear fusion—"God is a sun."

Part 2: Exploring the Dwelling Place

Our journey continues around the porch pillars of the eternal dwelling place of Light in which the Father, Son, and Spirit indwell One Another in fusion Oneness. Eric leads us through a clear understanding of "God is Light" and "God is a sun and shield" explaining the vortex of the Trinity and how we are called to be sharers of their holiness and mature children of Light.

Part 3: Revealing the Secret of the Mystery

This volume focuses on Pillar 8, "God in Christ," where we discover the secret mystery of our participation in the dynamic of the kingdom—the fusion of the Triune-God and regenerated sons and daughters dwelling together in the God-Man Jesus.

Part 4: Awakening to Spiritual Reality

This volume focuses on Pillar 9, "God is Spirit," where we discover how Father, Son, and Spirit fuse into One Another as a whirlwind. The Triune-Spirit created individual human beings as a tri-unity—spirit, soul, and body. We will learn how as free individuals we are fused by *Agape* into the Triune-Spirit.

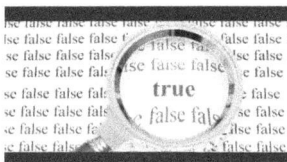

Part 5: Discerning "The Truth"

This volume focuses on Pillar 10, "God is true," revealing a deeper understanding of the divine nature of *Agape*—the "true" Love by which Father, Son, and Spirit abide in perpetual fusion as one God. We will discover how truth is in Jesus and how we by His grace becomes sharers of that truth. By carefully examining and receiving this truth, which the Triune-God desires to plant, cultivate, and mature within us, we are made capable of participating in a relationship of reciprocal generosity with Father, Son, Spirit and one another—the kingdom of God.

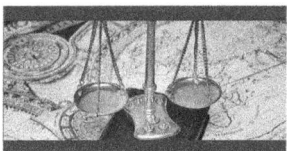

Part 6: Appraising the Most High

"O magnify the Lord with me!" (Ps. 34:3). One effective way to closely examine and worth-ship God is to meditate on what the Scriptures specifically testify that "God is." As the Holy Spirit progressively opens the *God is* statements of the Bible to us, we discover the fusion of the

Trinity. In this sixth volume, we continue investigating "God is true" (John 3:33) to discover why Father, Son, and Spirit, together are "the Most High God" (Ps. 78:35; Heb. 7:1). The Scriptures consistently use economic terms to describe how these three Eternals add to and exalt One Another by sacrifical Self-giving. The economy of the kingdom functions by giving and receiving in order to give again, which yields superabundant bounty. When we "exchanged the truth of God for the lie" (Rom. 1:25), we fell out of the abundant life of the Most High and bought into the corrupt economy of the world that operates by buying and selling one another for self-indulgence, which precipitates famine.

LIFECHANGERS®

P.O. Box 3709 ❖ Cookeville, TN 38502
931.520.3730 ❖ lc@lifechangers.org

www.ingramcontent.com/pod-product-compliance
Lightning Source LLC
Chambersburg PA
CBHW061732020426
42331CB00006B/1211